The
NYSTROM
WORLD
ATLAS

ΙꝊ NYSTROM Division of Herff Jones, Inc.

CREDITS

Atlas Design .... Matthew V. Kania

Project Director .... Joan Pederson

Production Manager .... Christine Bosacki

Executive Editor .... Charles Novosad

Managing Editor .... Ruth Koval

Nystrom Computer Cartography and Graphics ..... Bonnie Jones, Charlaine Wilkerson

Other Nystrom Cartography and Illustration .... Louise Feeney, James Franklin, Phyllis Kawano, Gerald Keefe, Michael Nauert, Julsun Pacheco

Additional Computer Cartography .... Maryland CartoGraphics, Inc.

Cover Design .... The Quarasan Group, Inc.

Photographic Research .... Charlotte Goldman

Consultants .... John R. Chalk, Principal, Templeton Secondary School, Vancouver, British Columbia

Ted Curtis, Social Studies Coordinator, Davenport Community Schools, Davenport, Iowa

PHOTO CREDITS

front cover *top*: Don Smetzer/Tony Stone Images; *left to right*: Andy Sacks/Tony Stone Images; Eric Meola/The Image Bank; John Lamb/Tony Stone Images **back cover**: Vic Bider/Tony Stone Images **11** *clockwise from top left*: William McKinney/FPG International; Mark Henley/Visuals Unlimited; H. Richard Johnston/Tony Stone Images; Paul A. Osman; John Warden/Tony Stone Images; Lionel Isy-Schwart/The Image Bank; Richard Thom/Visuals Unlimited **20** Lee Kuhn/FPG International **21** Mike Vines/Tony Stone Images **23** Eric Meola/The Image Bank **28** Gerald L. French/FPG International **30** Andy Sacks/Tony Stone Images **33** *clockwise from top left*: Paul Kenward/Tony Stone Images; Vic Bider/Tony Stone Images; John Scowen/FPG International; Pete Saloutos/Tony Stone Images **39** Juergen Vogt/The Image Bank **45** Albert J. Copley/Visuals Unlimited **49** Philip and Karen Smith/Tony Stone Images **55** Jon Womack **56** Albert J. Copley/Visuals Unlimited **57** Joachim Messerschmidt/Tony Stone Images **59** John Lamb/Tony Stone Images **62** Robert Frerck/Tony Stone Images **63** John Ferner/Visuals Unlimited **70** Tony Stone Images **72** G. Prance/Visuals Unlimited **73** Charles Gupton/Tony Stone Images **74** Tim Hauf/Visuals Unlimited **80** Penny Tweedie/Tony Stone Images **81** *from left*: Ronald Gordon/Tony Stone Images; W. Fischer/FPG International **82** Tony Stone Images

UNITS OF MEASUREMENT

This atlas gives measurements in metric units as well as the customary units of the United States. The U.S. spelling of metric units differs from the international style. For example, it is *meter* in the United States and *metre* in Canada. There are many other small differences in the two styles. One is in the shortening of such phrases as "per square kilometer." Often abbreviated as *per sq. km* in the United States, it is shown as km^2 in Canada. The symbols for metric units, however, are the same in both styles.

ISBN: 0-88463-480-9
10 9 8 7   99 98 97 96

Printed in U.S.A. • Product Code Number 9A90

For information about ordering this atlas, call toll-free 800-621-8086.

CONTENTS

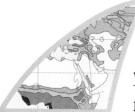

The *Nystrom World Atlas* includes both physical and political reference maps, which provide general information on major regions, as well as a variety of special maps. Each has its own map legend or key.

The atlas also includes graphs, photographs, and drawings. At the end of the book, an index describes places named on the maps and tells where they are located.

PHYSICAL MAPS

Physical reference maps in the atlas use color to show land elevations and water depths. They name many landforms and bodies of water, and also countries and selected cities. Areas that are not part of the map's subject are shown in a neutral color.

ELEVATION COLORS

For each physical map there is a short legend that includes a key to the map's colors. Elevations and depths are given in both meters and feet. the complete legend for all the reference maps is on page 5.

POLITICAL MAPS

Political reference maps in the atlas use color to show where one country or state ends and another begins. They name many more cities than physical maps and also name rivers, lakes, and major water bodies. Nonsubject areas have a neutral color.

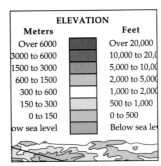

DIRECTION ARROWS AND MAP GRID

All reference maps in the atlas have compass arrows that point in the cardinal directions. True north, south, east, or west are always found by following the map's grid lines. The latitude or longitude of each line in the map grid is identified.

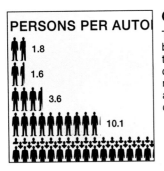

SPECIAL MAPS

In addition to the reference maps, the atlas has various special maps of the world's regions. These are often called thematic maps because each focuses on a single subject, or theme.

SPECIAL MAP KEYS

Every special map has a key to explain its symbols, which in most cases are colors. The same colors can stand for population densities on one map, growing seasons on a second map, and land uses on a third. That is why it is important to read the key before using the map.

GRAPHS

The atlas includes circle graphs, bar graphs, line graphs, and pictographs. Graphs summarize complex facts in a visual way, making it easier to see similarities and differences among countries of the world.

PROJECTIONS

Map projections are the means by which the curved surface of a globe is transferred to the flat surface of a map. Some of the infinite number of possible projections are explained on pages 84 and 85. Robinson, Eckert IV, and Miller are among the projections used in this atlas.

PHOTOGRAPHS AND DRAWINGS

The numerous photographs in the atlas help show the characteristics of places around the world. Special drawings are used to illustrate things that are difficult to see in a photograph or map.

INDEX

The index lists many of the places that are named on various maps in the atlas. Each place is briefly described. A page number and latitude-longitude location tell where it can be found.

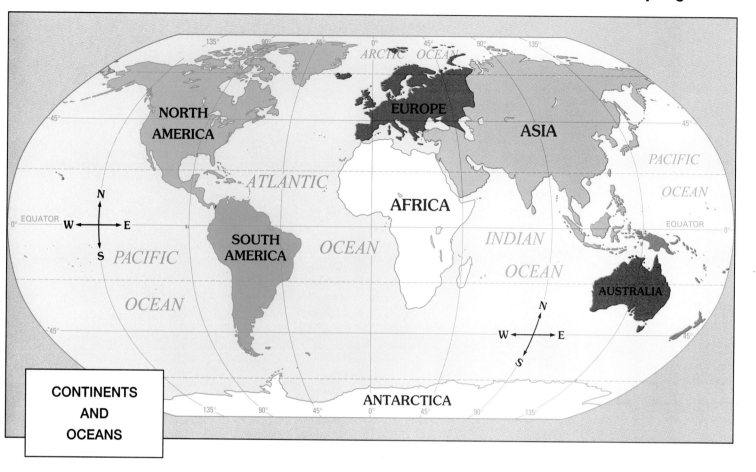

CONTINENTS
AND
OCEANS

LEGEND FOR PHYSICAL AND POLITICAL REFERENCE MAPS

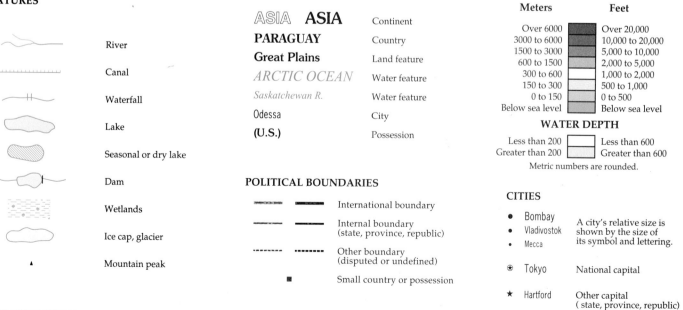

LAND AND WATER FEATURES

River

Canal

Waterfall

Lake

Seasonal or dry lake

Dam

Wetlands

Ice cap, glacier

▲ Mountain peak

LETTERING STYLES

ASIA **ASIA** Continent

PARAGUAY Country

Great Plains Land feature

ARCTIC OCEAN Water feature

Saskatchewan R. Water feature

Odessa City

(U.S.) Possession

POLITICAL BOUNDARIES

International boundary

Internal boundary
(state, province, republic)

Other boundary
(disputed or undefined)

■ Small country or possession

ELEVATION

Meters		Feet
Over 6000		Over 20,000
3000 to 6000		10,000 to 20,000
1500 to 3000		5,000 to 10,000
600 to 1500		2,000 to 5,000
300 to 600		1,000 to 2,000
150 to 300		500 to 1,000
0 to 150		0 to 500
Below sea level		Below sea level

WATER DEPTH

Less than 200		Less than 600
Greater than 200		Greater than 600

Metric numbers are rounded.

CITIES

● Bombay

• Vladivostok

· Mecca

A city's relative size is shown by the size of its symbol and lettering.

⊛ Tokyo National capital

★ Hartford Other capital
(state, province, republic)

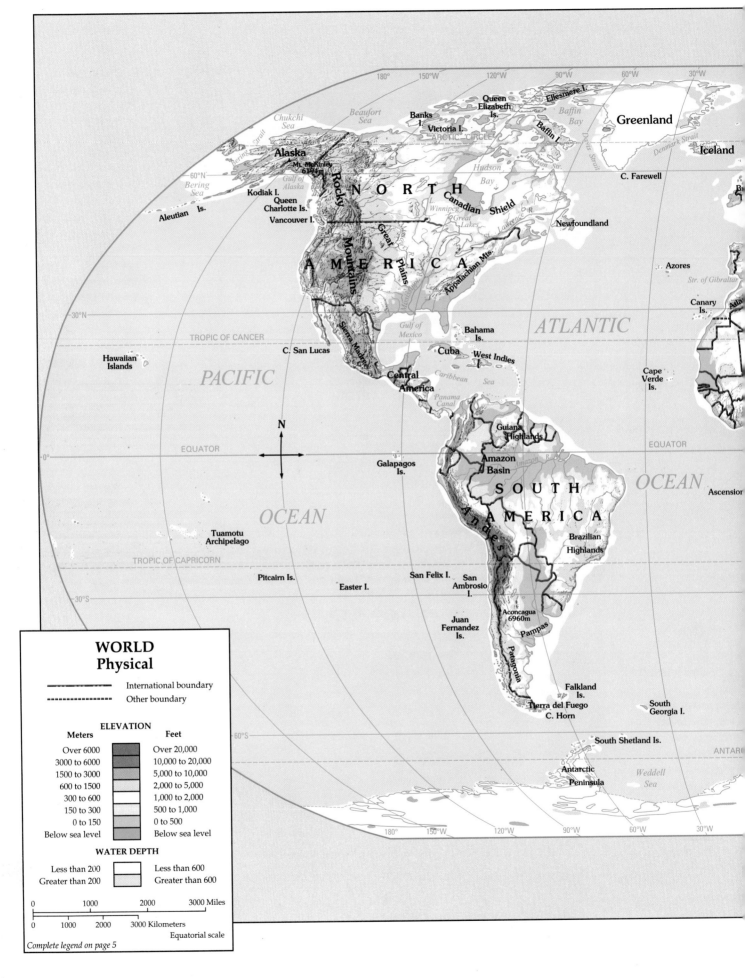

WORLD
Physical

———————— International boundary
- - - - - - - - - Other boundary

ELEVATION

Meters		Feet
Over 6000		Over 20,000
3000 to 6000		10,000 to 20,000
1500 to 3000		5,000 to 10,000
600 to 1500		2,000 to 5,000
300 to 600		1,000 to 2,000
150 to 300		500 to 1,000
0 to 150		0 to 500
Below sea level		Below sea level

WATER DEPTH

Less than 200		Less than 600
Greater than 200		Greater than 600

0   1000   2000   3000 Miles

0   1000   2000   3000 Kilometers

Equatorial scale

Complete legend on page 5

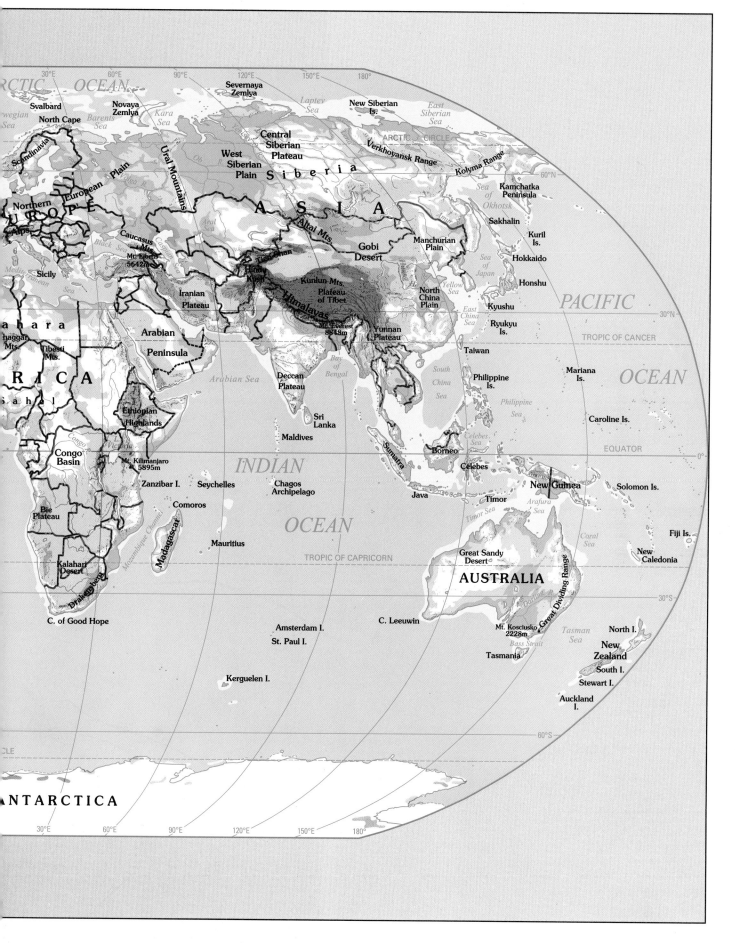

ARCTIC OCEAN

Svalbard
North Cape
Novaya
Zemlya
Severnaya
Zemlya
New Siberian
Is.
Laptev
Sea
East
Siberian
Sea
ARCTIC CIRCLE

Norwegian
Sea
Barents
Sea
Kara
Sea
Central
Siberian
Plateau
Verkhoyansk Range
Kolyma Range
60°N

Scandinavia
West
Siberian
Plain
S i b e r i a
Kamchatka
Peninsula
Sea
of
Okhotsk

European Plain
Ural Mountains
A S I A
Sakhalin
Kuril
Is.

EUROPE
Alps
Ob
Aral
Sea
Altai Mts.
Manchurian
Plain
Sea
of
Japan
Hokkaido

Northern
Caucasus
Mts.
Mt. Elbus
5642m
Caspian Sea
Tian Shan
Gobi
Desert
Honshu

Black Sea
Hindu
Kush
Kunlun Mts.
Plateau
of Tibet
North
China
Plain
Yellow
Sea
Kyushu
PACIFIC

Sicily
Mediterranean Sea
Iranian
Plateau
Himalayas
Huang
Ryukyu
Is.
30°N

Sahara
Arabian
Peninsula
Mt. Everest
8848m
Yunnan
Plateau
East
China
Sea
TROPIC OF CANCER

Ahaggar
Mts.
Tibesti
Mts.
Arabian Sea
Deccan
Plateau
Taiwan
Mariana
Is.
OCEAN

AFRICA
Sahel
Ethiopian
Highlands
Sri
Lanka
South
China
Sea
Philippine
Is.

Congo
Maldives
Bay
of
Bengal
Philippine
Sea
Caroline Is.

INDIAN
Chagos
Archipelago
Sumatra
Borneo
Celebes
Sea
EQUATOR
0°

Congo
Basin
Mt. Kilimanjaro
5895m
L. Victoria
Seychelles
Java
Celebes
New Guinea
Solomon Is.

Zanzibar I.
OCEAN
Timor
Arafura
Sea

Bie
Plateau
Comoros
Madagascar
Mozambique Channel
Timor Sea
Coral
Sea
Fiji Is.

Mauritius
TROPIC OF CAPRICORN
Great Sandy
Desert
New
Caledonia

Kalahari
Desert
Drakensberg
AUSTRALIA
Great Dividing Range
30°S

C. of Good Hope
Amsterdam I.
St. Paul I.
C. Leeuwin
Mt. Kosciusko
2228m
Darling
Tasman
Sea
North I.
New
Zealand

Kerguelen I.
Tasmania
Bass Strait
South I.
Stewart I.

Auckland
I.

60°S

ANTARCTICA

30°E   60°E   90°E   120°E   150°E   180°

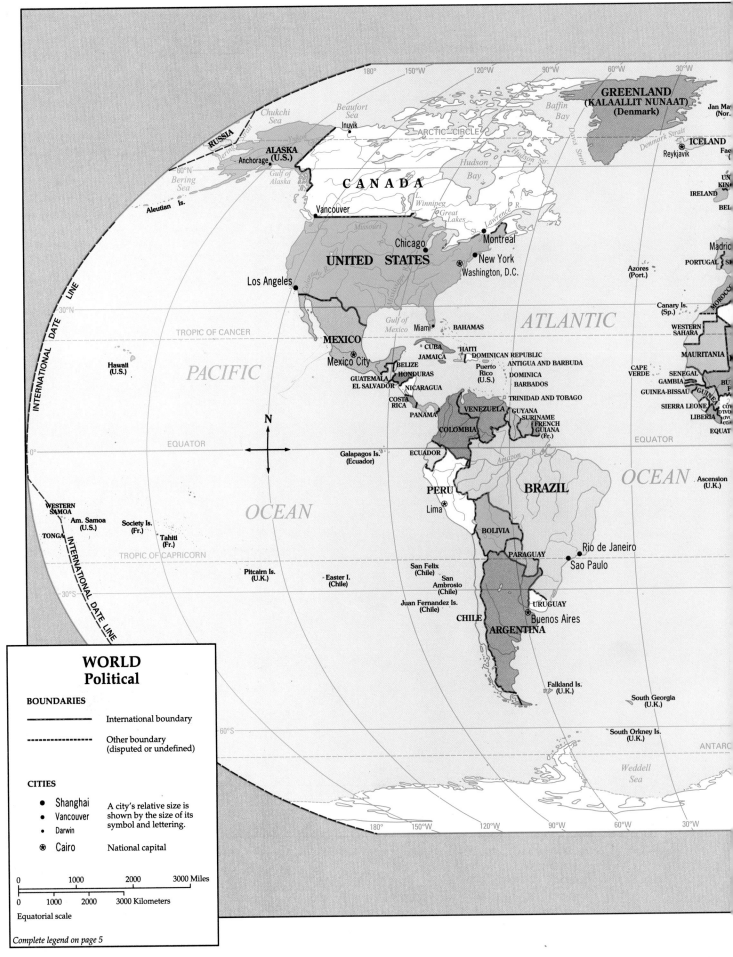

WORLD
Political

BOUNDARIES

—————————— International boundary

- - - - - - - - - Other boundary
(disputed or undefined)

CITIES

● Shanghai   A city's relative size is
shown by the size of its
● Vancouver   symbol and lettering.
∙ Darwin

⊛ Cairo   National capital

0   1000   2000   3000 Miles

0   1000   2000   3000 Kilometers

Equatorial scale

Complete legend on page 5

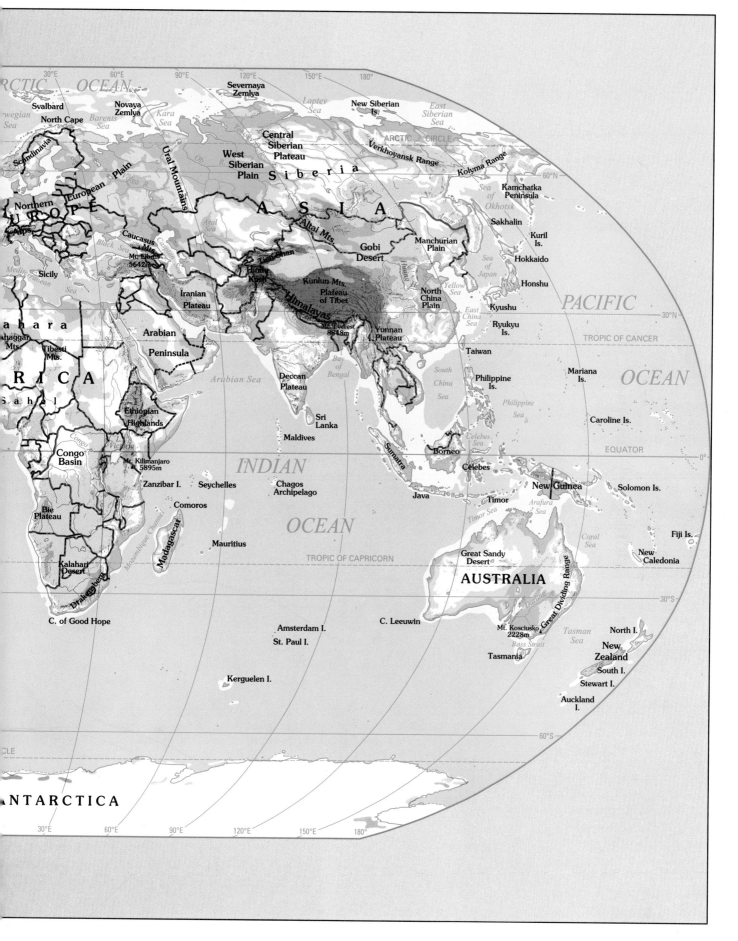

ARCTIC OCEAN
30°E   60°E   90°E   120°E   150°E   180°

Svalbard
North Cape
Novaya Zemlya
Severnaya Zemlya
Kara Sea
Laptev Sea
New Siberian Is.
East Siberian Sea
ARCTIC CIRCLE

Barents Sea

Scandinavia
European Plain
West Siberian Plain
Central Siberian Plateau
Siberia
Verkhoyansk Range
Kolyma Range
60°N

EUROPE
Northern
Alps
Caucasus Mts.
Mt. Elbrus 5642m
Black Sea
Caspian Sea
Aral Sea
A S I A
Altai Mts.
Gobi Desert
Manchurian Plain
Kamchatka Peninsula
Sea of Okhotsk
Sakhalin
Kuril Is.
Hokkaido

Mediterranean Sea
Sicily
Iranian Plateau
Tien Shan
Hindu Kush
Kunlun Mts.
Plateau of Tibet
Himalayas
Mt. Everest 8848m
North China Plain
Amur
Huang
Sea of Japan
Honshu
Kyushu
Yellow Sea
East China Sea
Ryukyu Is.
PACIFIC
30°N

Sahara
Ahaggar Mts.
Tibesti Mts.
Arabian Peninsula
Yunnan Plateau
Taiwan
TROPIC OF CANCER

AFRICA
Sahel
Arabian Sea
Deccan Plateau
Bay of Bengal
South China Sea
Philippine Is.
Philippine Sea
Mariana Is.
OCEAN

Ethiopian Highlands
Sri Lanka
Maldives
Caroline Is.

Congo
Congo Basin
Lake Victoria
Mt. Kilimanjaro 5895m
Zanzibar I.
Seychelles
Chagos Archipelago
INDIAN
Sumatra
Borneo
Celebes Sea
Celebes
Java
New Guinea
Arafura Sea
Timor
Solomon Is.
EQUATOR
0°

Bie Plateau
Comoros
Mauritius
OCEAN
Timor Sea
Coral Sea
Fiji Is.
New Caledonia

Mozambique Channel
Madagascar
Great Sandy Desert
AUSTRALIA
Great Dividing Range
TROPIC OF CAPRICORN

Kalahari Desert
Drakensberg
C. of Good Hope
Amsterdam I.
St. Paul I.
C. Leeuwin
Mt. Kosciusko 2228m
Tasman Sea
Bass Strait
North I.
New Zealand
South I.
Stewart I.
30°S

Tasmania
Kerguelen I.
Auckland I.
60°S

ANTARCTICA
CIRCLE
30°E   60°E   90°E   120°E   150°E   180°

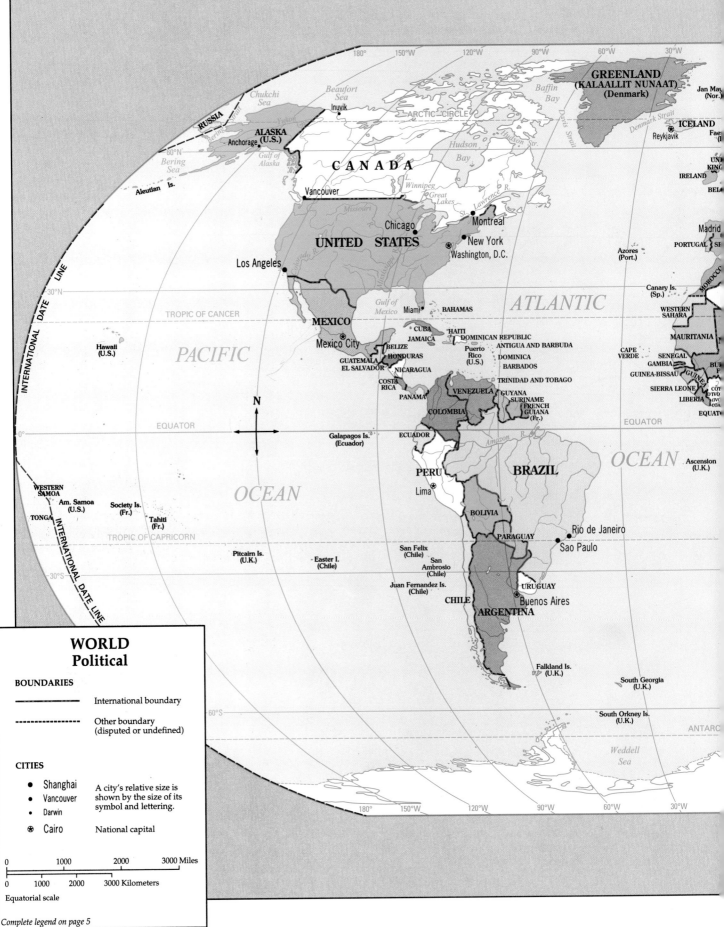

WORLD
Political

BOUNDARIES

International boundary

Other boundary
(disputed or undefined)

CITIES

● Shanghai — A city's relative size is shown by the size of its symbol and lettering.

● Vancouver

● Darwin

⊛ Cairo — National capital

0   1000   2000   3000 Miles

0   1000   2000   3000 Kilometers

Equatorial scale

Complete legend on page 5

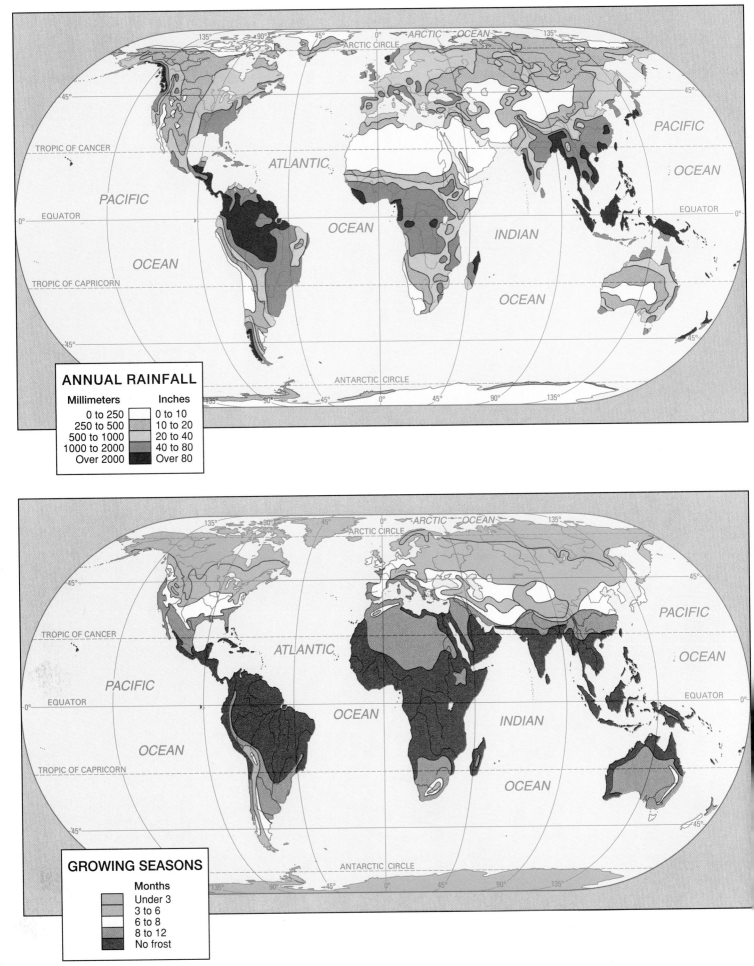

ANNUAL RAINFALL

Millimeters		Inches
0 to 250		0 to 10
250 to 500		10 to 20
500 to 1000		20 to 40
1000 to 2000		40 to 80
Over 2000		Over 80

GROWING SEASONS

Months
Under 3
3 to 6
6 to 8
8 to 12
No frost

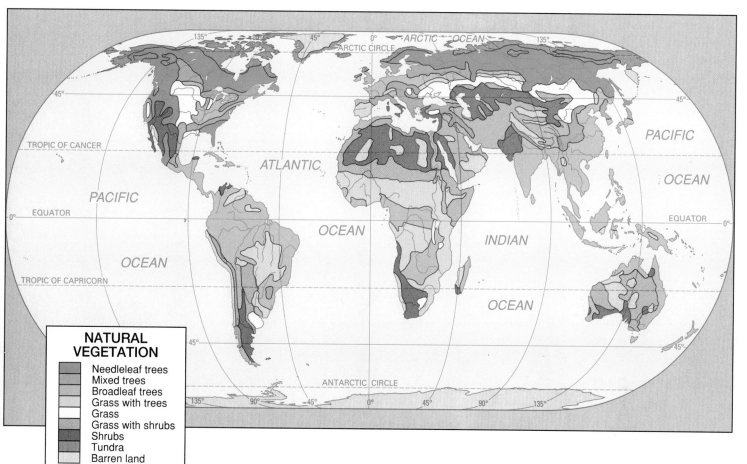

NATURAL VEGETATION

- Needleleaf trees
- Mixed trees
- Broadleaf trees
- Grass with trees
- Grass
- Grass with shrubs
- Shrubs
- Tundra
- Barren land

Needleleaf trees

Mixed trees

Broadleaf trees

Grass with trees

TYPES OF VEGETATION

The world can be divided into zones of natural vegetation. Several categories of vegetation are mapped above.

Most of the categories could be subdivided. For example, there are several kinds of broadleaf trees: maples, oaks, birches, sycamores, cottonwoods, and so on.

Seven types of vegetation listed in the map key are shown here.

Grass

Shrubs

Tundra

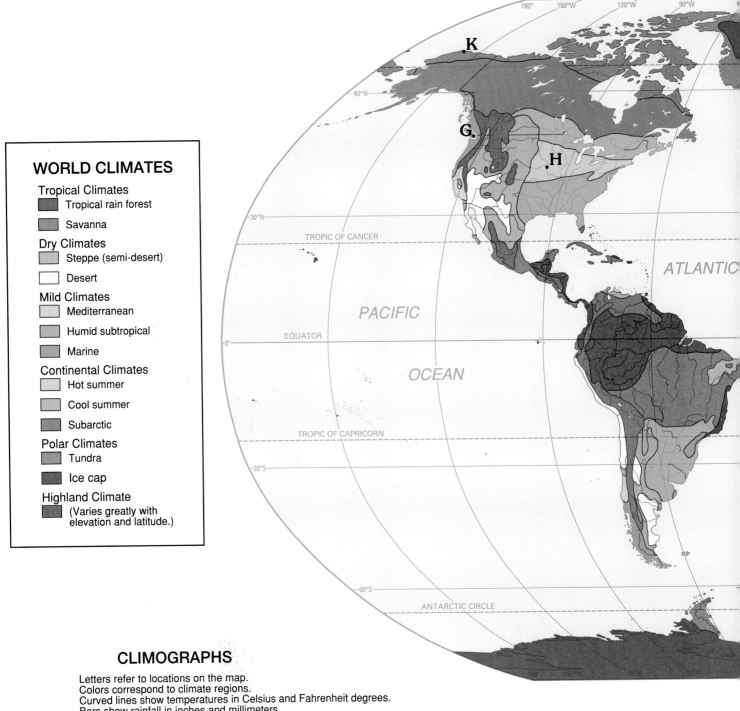

WORLD CLIMATES

Tropical Climates
- Tropical rain forest
- Savanna

Dry Climates
- Steppe (semi-desert)
- Desert

Mild Climates
- Mediterranean
- Humid subtropical
- Marine

Continental Climates
- Hot summer
- Cool summer
- Subarctic

Polar Climates
- Tundra
- Ice cap

Highland Climate
- (Varies greatly with elevation and latitude.)

ATLANTIC

PACIFIC

OCEAN

TROPIC OF CANCER

EQUATOR

TROPIC OF CAPRICORN

ANTARCTIC CIRCLE

CLIMOGRAPHS

Letters refer to locations on the map.
Colors correspond to climate regions.
Curved lines show temperatures in Celsius and Fahrenheit degrees.
Bars show rainfall in inches and millimeters.

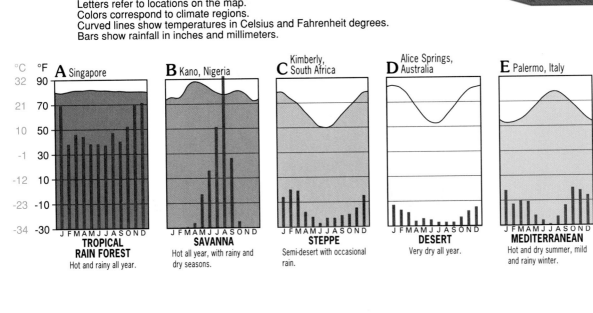

A Singapore
TROPICAL RAIN FOREST
Hot and rainy all year.

B Kano, Nigeria
SAVANNA
Hot all year, with rainy and dry seasons.

C Kimberly, South Africa
STEPPE
Semi-desert with occasional rain.

D Alice Springs, Australia
DESERT
Very dry all year.

E Palermo, Italy
MEDITERRANEAN
Hot and dry summer, mild and rainy winter.

F Hankou, China
HUMID SUBTROPICAL
Hot and wet summer, mild and damp winter.

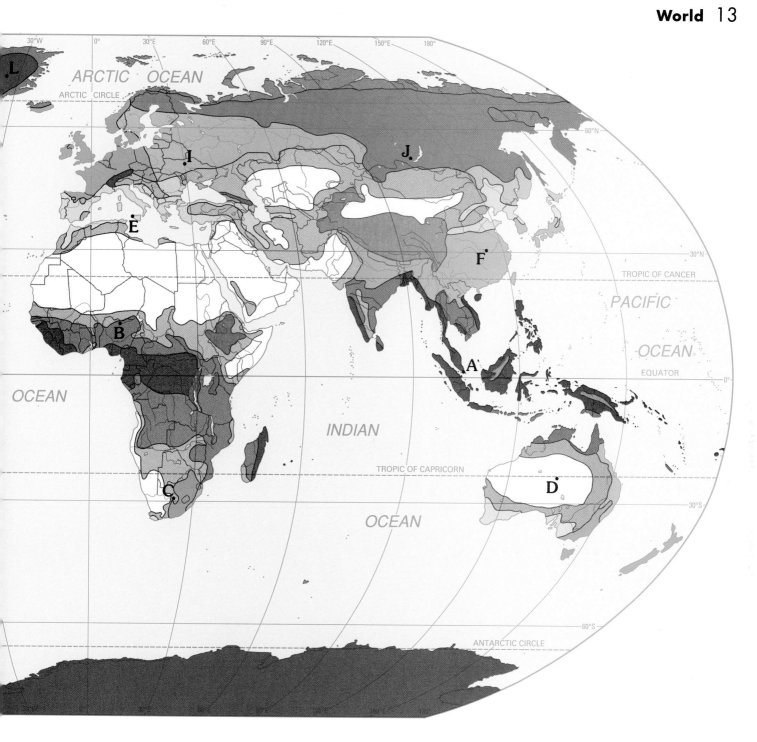

ARCTIC OCEAN

ARCTIC CIRCLE

PACIFIC OCEAN

INDIAN OCEAN

OCEAN

TROPIC OF CANCER

EQUATOR

TROPIC OF CAPRICORN

ANTARCTIC CIRCLE

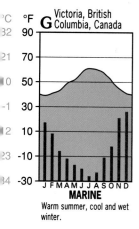

°C °F **G** Victoria, British Columbia, Canada

32 90
21 70
0 50
-1 30
10
-23 -10
-34 -30

J F M A M J J A S O N D

MARINE

Warm summer, cool and wet winter.

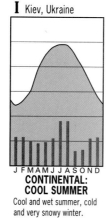

H Omaha, Nebraska, United States

J F M A M J J A S O N D

CONTINENTAL: HOT SUMMER

Hot and wet summer, cold and snowy winter.

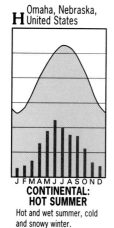

I Kiev, Ukraine

J F M A M J J A S O N D

CONTINENTAL: COOL SUMMER

Cool and wet summer, cold and very snowy winter.

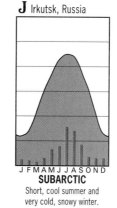

J Irkutsk, Russia

J F M A M J J A S O N D

SUBARCTIC

Short, cool summer and very cold, snowy winter.

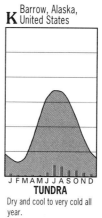

K Barrow, Alaska, United States

J F M A M J J A S O N D

TUNDRA

Dry and cool to very cold all year.

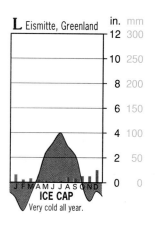

L Eismitte, Greenland

in. mm
12 300
10 250
8 200
6 150
4 100
2 50
0 0

J F M A M J J A S O N D

ICE CAP

Very cold all year.

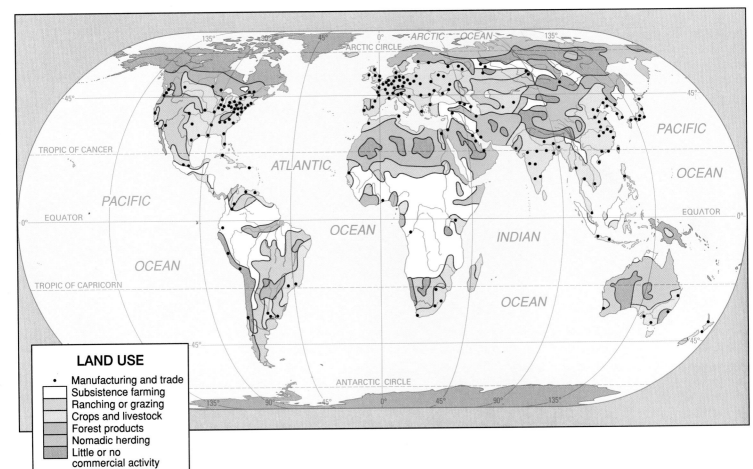

LAND USE

- Manufacturing and trade
- Subsistence farming
- Ranching or grazing
- Crops and livestock
- Forest products
- Nomadic herding
- Little or no commercial activity

CORN

Corn, also called maize, is one of the world's most important grain crops. The chief corn-growing nation is the United States. Other major producers include China, Brazil, and Russia. Corn is eaten by both people and livestock, and corn syrup is widely used as a sweetener in soft drinks and packaged foods. Corn also is used in the manufacture of medicines, paper goods, and other products.

WHEAT

The grain from this member of the grass family is used to make wheat flour, which is the main ingredient in most breads, many breakfast foods, and such pasta dishes such as spaghetti and macaroni. Wheat also is used as feed for livestock. The leading wheat producer is China, followed by the United States, India, and Russia.

SOYBEAN

Also known as soya or soja bean, this plant is a cheap source of protein and vegetable oil in the human diet. Soybeans also are used in livestock feed and as a raw material by industry. The United States grows two-thirds of the world's soybeans. Brazil and China also are major producers.

RICE

Rice is the main food for over half the people of the world. In many parts of Asia, rice is eaten three times a day and is far more important than wheat is in North America. China, India, Indonesia, and other Asian countries are the leading rice producers. Rice requires a warm climate with heavy rainfall or a constant supply of water.

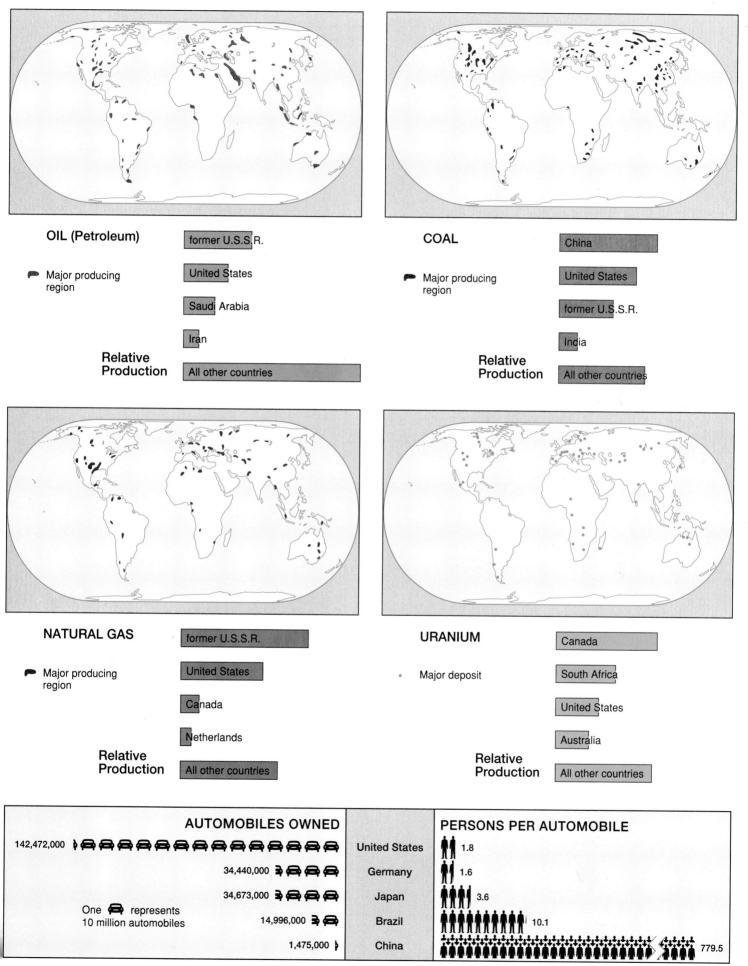

OIL (Petroleum)

🖐 Major producing region

| former U.S.S.R. |
| United States |
| Saudi Arabia |
| Iran |

Relative Production

| All other countries |

COAL

🖐 Major producing region

| China |
| United States |
| former U.S.S.R. |
| India |

Relative Production

| All other countries |

NATURAL GAS

🖐 Major producing region

| former U.S.S.R. |
| United States |
| Canada |
| Netherlands |

Relative Production

| All other countries |

URANIUM

• Major deposit

| Canada |
| South Africa |
| United States |
| Australia |

Relative Production

| All other countries |

AUTOMOBILES OWNED

142,472,000	United States
34,440,000	Germany
34,673,000	Japan
14,996,000	Brazil
1,475,000	China

One 🚗 represents 10 million automobiles

PERSONS PER AUTOMOBILE

United States	1.8
Germany	1.6
Japan	3.6
Brazil	10.1
China	779.5

WORLD POPULATION

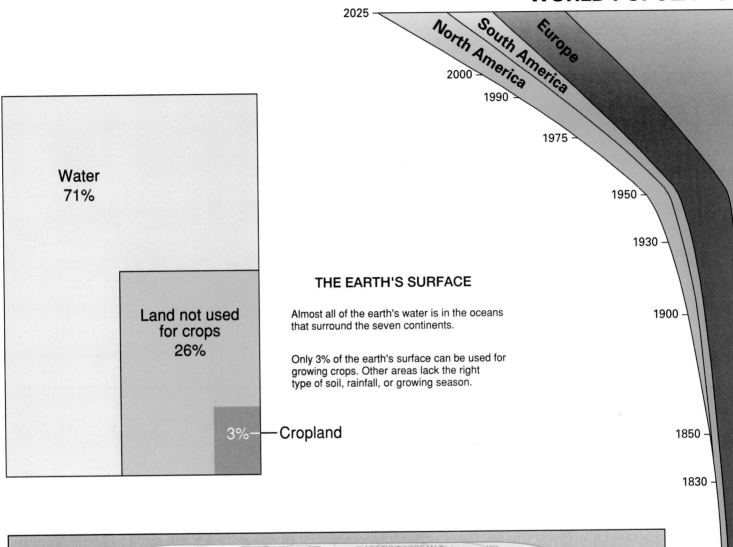

Water
71%

Land not used
for crops
26%

3% — Cropland

THE EARTH'S SURFACE

Almost all of the earth's water is in the oceans
that surround the seven continents.

Only 3% of the earth's surface can be used for
growing crops. Other areas lack the right
type of soil, rainfall, or growing season.

2025
2000
1990
1975
1950
1930
1900
1850
1830
1800
1750
1700
Year 1650 -

North America
South America
Europe

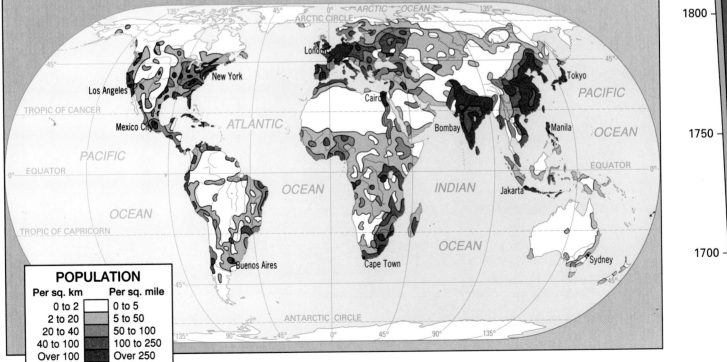

POPULATION

Per sq. km	Per sq. mile
0 to 2	0 to 5
2 to 20	5 to 50
20 to 40	50 to 100
40 to 100	100 to 250
Over 100	Over 250

GROWTH 1650-2025

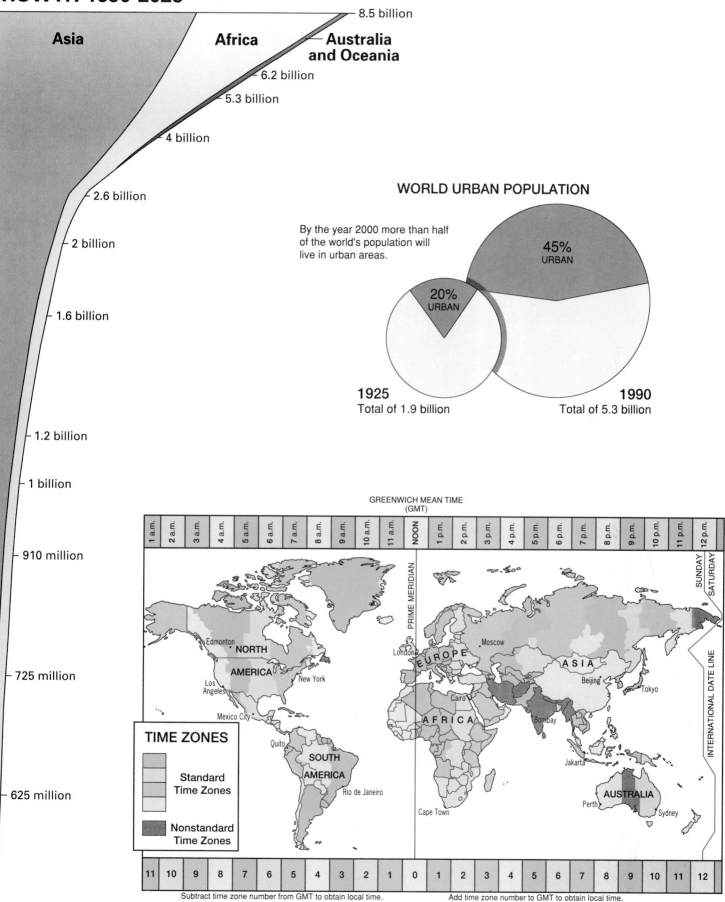

Asia **Africa** **Australia and Oceania**

- 8.5 billion
- 6.2 billion
- 5.3 billion
- 4 billion
- 2.6 billion
- 2 billion
- 1.6 billion
- 1.2 billion
- 1 billion
- 910 million
- 725 million
- 625 million
- 550 million

WORLD URBAN POPULATION

By the year 2000 more than half of the world's population will live in urban areas.

20% URBAN

45% URBAN

1925
Total of 1.9 billion

1990
Total of 5.3 billion

GREENWICH MEAN TIME
(GMT)

| 1 a.m. | 2 a.m. | 3 a.m. | 4 a.m. | 5 a.m. | 6 a.m. | 7 a.m. | 8 a.m. | 9 a.m. | 10 a.m. | 11 a.m. | NOON | 1 p.m. | 2 p.m. | 3 p.m. | 4 p.m. | 5 p.m. | 6 p.m. | 7 p.m. | 8 p.m. | 9 p.m. | 10 p.m. | 11 p.m. | 12 p.m. |

PRIME MERIDIAN

SUNDAY / SATURDAY

INTERNATIONAL DATE LINE

Edmonton
NORTH
AMERICA
New York
Los Angeles
Mexico City
Quito
SOUTH
AMERICA
Rio de Janeiro
London
EUROPE
Moscow
ASIA
Beijing
Tokyo
Cairo
AFRICA
Bombay
Jakarta
Cape Town
AUSTRALIA
Perth
Sydney

TIME ZONES

Standard Time Zones

Nonstandard Time Zones

| 11 | 10 | 9 | 8 | 7 | 6 | 5 | 4 | 3 | 2 | 1 | 0 | 1 | 2 | 3 | 4 | 5 | 6 | 7 | 8 | 9 | 10 | 11 | 12 |

Subtract time zone number from GMT to obtain local time.

Add time zone number to GMT to obtain local time.

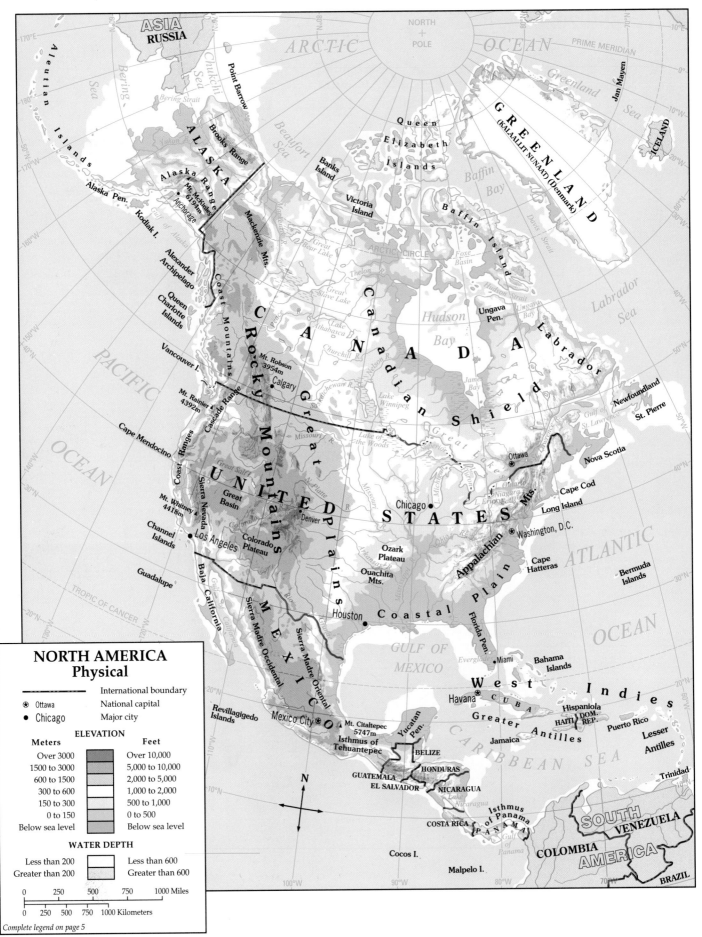

NORTH AMERICA
Physical

———————	International boundary
⊛ Ottawa	National capital
• Chicago	Major city

ELEVATION

Meters		Feet
Over 3000		Over 10,000
1500 to 3000		5,000 to 10,000
600 to 1500		2,000 to 5,000
300 to 600		1,000 to 2,000
150 to 300		500 to 1,000
0 to 150		0 to 500
Below sea level		Below sea level

WATER DEPTH

Less than 200		Less than 600
Greater than 200		Greater than 600

0   250   500   750   1000 Miles

0   250   500   750 1000 Kilometers

Complete legend on page 5

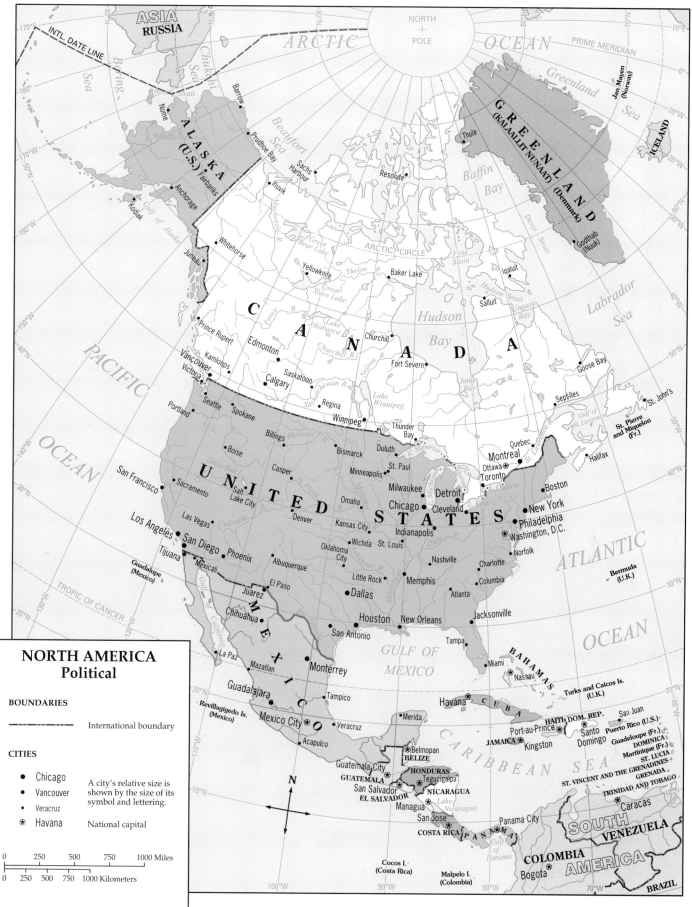

ASIA
RUSSIA
ARCTIC
NORTH + POLE
OCEAN
PRIME MERIDIAN
INTL. DATE LINE
Chukchi Sea
Beaufort Sea
Greenland
Jan Mayen (Norway)
Sea
Barrow
Nome
ALASKA (U.S.)
Fairbanks
Prudhoe Bay
Sachs Harbour
Resolute
Baffin Bay
G R E E N L A N D (KALAALLIT NUNAAT) (Denmark)
Thule
ICELAND
Bering Strait
Yukon
Anchorage
Inuvik
Kodiak
Gulf of Alaska
Whitehorse
ARCTIC CIRCLE
Foxe Basin
Iqaluit
Juneau
Yellowknife
Great Bear Lake
Baker Lake
Thelon R.
Hudson Strait
Salluit
Ungava Bay
Labrador Sea
Prince Rupert
Great Slave Lake
C A N A D A
Peace R.
Edmonton
Athabasca R.
Churchill
Fort Severn
Hudson Bay
Goose Bay
Mackenzie R.
Vancouver
Kamloops
Saskatoon
Calgary
Nelson R.
Saskatchewan R.
Regina
James Bay
Sept-Iles
St. John's
Victoria
Churchill R.
Winnipeg
Lake Winnipeg
Gulf of St. Lawrence
Seattle
Spokane
Thunder Bay
Quebec
St. Pierre and Miquelon (Fr.)
Portland
Billings
Missouri R.
Duluth
Montreal
Halifax
Boise
Bismarck
St. Paul
L. Superior
Ottawa
Toronto
Lake Ontario
Boston
San Francisco
Casper
Minneapolis
L. Michigan
Milwaukee
Detroit
Cleveland
New York
Sacramento
Great Salt L.
Omaha
U N I T E D
Chicago
L. Erie
Philadelphia
Salt Lake City
Denver
Platte R.
Kansas City
S T A T E S
Indianapolis
Washington, D.C.
Las Vegas
Colorado R.
Wichita
St. Louis
Ohio R.
Norfolk
Los Angeles
Oklahoma City
Nashville
Charlotte
PACIFIC
San Diego
Phoenix
Albuquerque
Arkansas R.
Memphis
Columbia
ATLANTIC
Tijuana
Little Rock
Mexicali
El Paso
Dallas
Atlanta
Guadalupe (Mexico)
Juarez
Rio Grande
Houston
New Orleans
Jacksonville
TROPIC OF CANCER
Chihuahua
San Antonio
OCEAN
M E X I C O
Tampa
Miami
Bermuda (U.K.)
La Paz
Monterrey
GULF OF MEXICO
BAHAMAS
Mazatlan
Nassau
Guadalajara
Tampico
Havana
C U B A
Turks and Caicos Is. (U.K.)
Revillagigedo Is. (Mexico)
Merida
San Juan
Mexico City
Veracruz
HAITI
DOM. REP.
Puerto Rico (U.S.)
Acapulco
Port-au-Prince
Santo Domingo
Guadeloupe (Fr.)
JAMAICA
Kingston
DOMINICA
Belmopan
MARTINIQUE (Fr.)
BELIZE
HONDURAS
ST. LUCIA
N
Guatemala City
Tegucigalpa
ST. VINCENT AND THE GRENADINES
GRENADA
GUATEMALA
NICARAGUA
TRINIDAD AND TOBAGO
San Salvador
EL SALVADOR
Lake Nicaragua
Caracas
Managua
C A R I B B E A N   S E A
San Jose
Panama City
SOUTH
VENEZUELA
Cocos I. (Costa Rica)
COSTA RICA
P A N A M A
Gulf of Panama
COLOMBIA
AMERICA
Malpelo I. (Colombia)
Bogota
BRAZIL
170°E   180°   170°W   160°W   150°W   140°W   130°W   120°W   110°W   100°W   90°W   80°W   70°W   60°W   50°W   40°W   30°W   20°W   10°W   0°   10°E
70°N   60°N   50°N   40°N   30°N   20°N   10°N

**NORTH AMERICA
Political**

BOUNDARIES

——————— International boundary

CITIES

● Chicago

• Vancouver

· Veracruz

⊛ Havana

A city's relative size is shown by the size of its symbol and lettering.

National capital

0   250   500   750   1000 Miles

0 250 500 750 1000 Kilometers

Complete legend on page 5

GROWING SEASONS

Months
- Under 3
- 3 to 6
- 6 to 8
- 8 to 12
- No frost

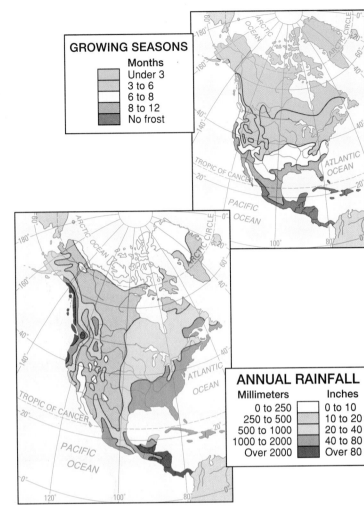

ANNUAL RAINFALL

Millimeters	Inches
0 to 250	0 to 10
250 to 500	10 to 20
500 to 1000	20 to 40
1000 to 2000	40 to 80
Over 2000	Over 80

Mt. McKinley, in the Alaska Range, towers over its surroundings. At 20,320 feet (6197 m) it is the highest peak in North America.

GREAT LAKES

Lakes Superior, Huron, Ontario, Michigan, and Erie are known as the Great Lakes. All five are connected and form the most important inland waterway in North America. From the early 1800s on, they have been heavily used to transport raw materials and finished goods. Today many ships pass through the Great Lakes to the St. Lawrence and then travel that river to the Atlantic Ocean.

Surface elevation (height above sea level) varies from one lake to the next. The most dramatic difference is from Lake Erie to Lake Ontario, a drop that is spectacularly seen at Niagara Falls. A series of canals and water-filled chambers called *locks* raise and lower ships from one lake to another.

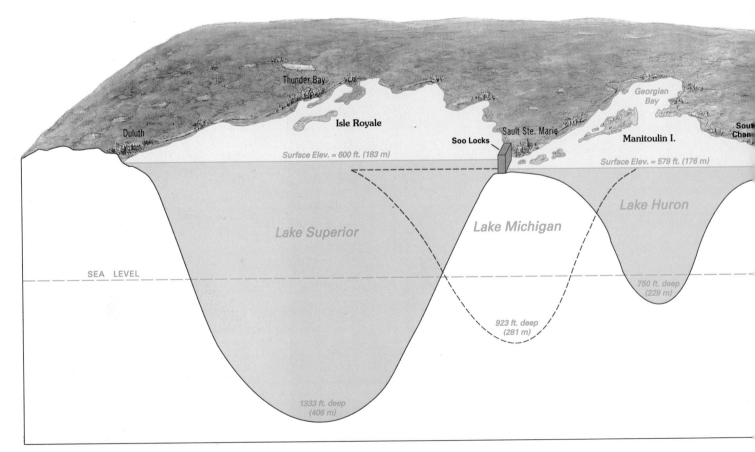

Niagara Falls on the Niagara River lies on both sides of the U.S.-Canadian border. A great tourist attraction, the falls are also a source of electrical power for the region.

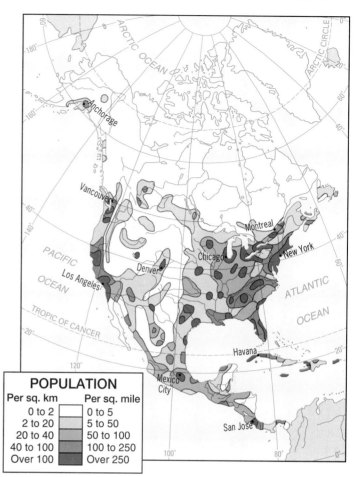

POPULATION

Per sq. km	Per sq. mile
0 to 2	0 to 5
2 to 20	5 to 50
20 to 40	50 to 100
40 to 100	100 to 250
Over 100	Over 250

CANADA

Thunder Bay
Lake Superior
Duluth
Sault Ste. Marie
Montreal
Ottawa
Lake Huron
Green Bay
Lake Michigan
Toronto
Milwaukee
UNITED
Hamilton
Lake Ontario
St. Lawrence River
Buffalo
STATES
Detroit
Windsor
Chicago
Lake Erie
Toledo
Cleveland

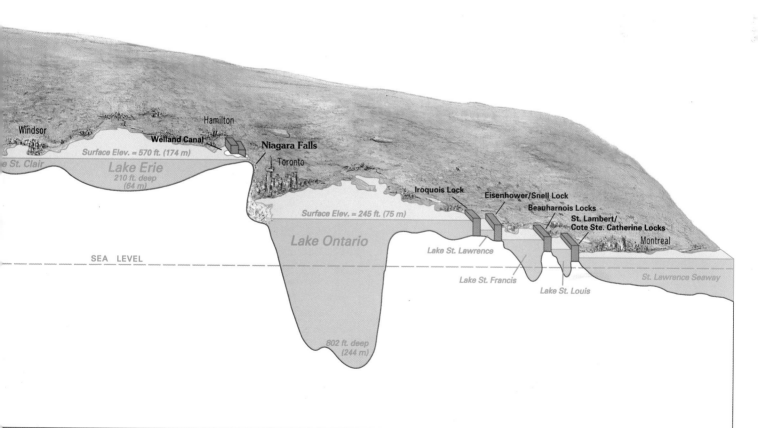

Windsor

Hamilton
Welland Canal
Niagara Falls
Surface Elev. = 570 ft. (174 m)
Toronto

e St. Clair
Lake Erie
210 ft. deep
(64 m)

Iroquois Lock
Eisenhower/Snell Lock
Beauharnois Locks
St. Lambert/
Cote Ste. Catherine Locks
Surface Elev. = 245 ft. (75 m)
Montreal

Lake Ontario

Lake St. Lawrence

SEA LEVEL

Lake St. Francis
Lake St. Louis
St. Lawrence Seaway

802 ft. deep
(244 m)

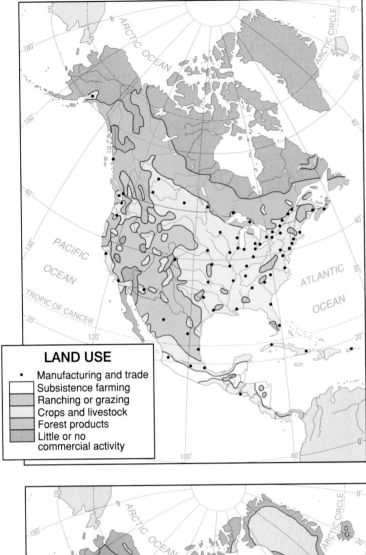

LAND USE

- • Manufacturing and trade
- Subsistence farming
- Ranching or grazing
- Crops and livestock
- Forest products
- Little or no commercial activity

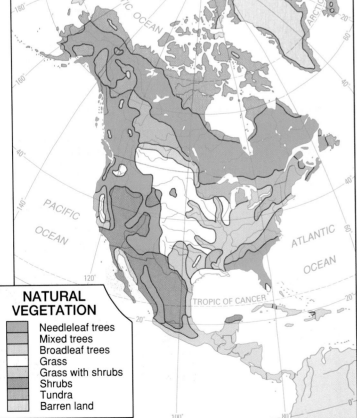

NATURAL VEGETATION

- Needleleaf trees
- Mixed trees
- Broadleaf trees
- Grass
- Grass with shrubs
- Shrubs
- Tundra
- Barren land

Giant sequoias are among the world's largest and oldest living things. They are found only on the west side of the Sierra Nevada, between 5,000 and 7,800 feet (1500 and 2400 m) above sea level. The largest of them is about 275 feet tall and 33 feet thick (84 and 10 m). Many are 2,000 to 3,000 years old.

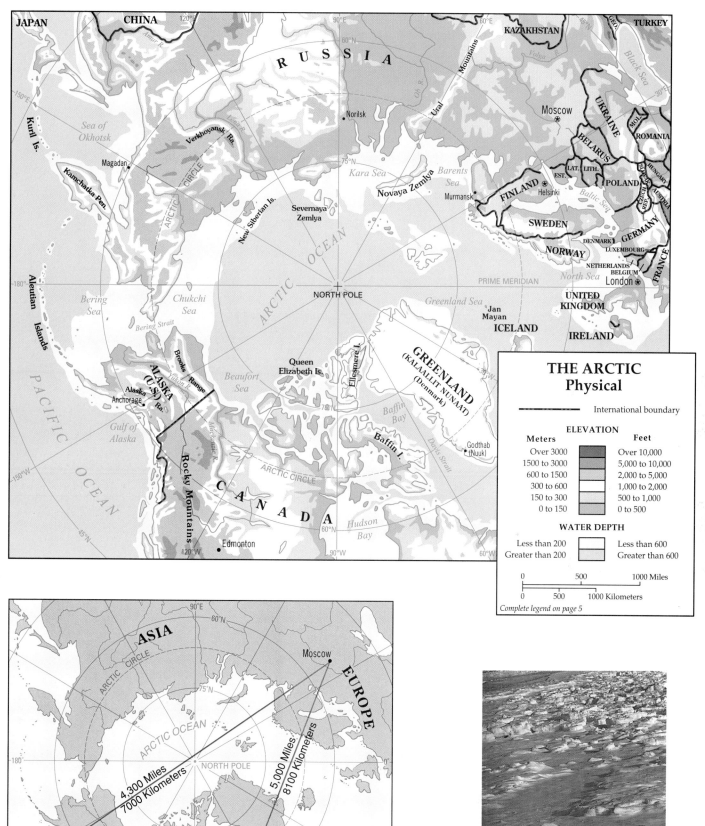

THE ARCTIC
Physical

——————— International boundary

ELEVATION

Meters		Feet
Over 3000		Over 10,000
1500 to 3000		5,000 to 10,000
600 to 1500		2,000 to 5,000
300 to 600		1,000 to 2,000
150 to 300		500 to 1,000
0 to 150		0 to 500

WATER DEPTH

Less than 200		Less than 600
Greater than 200		Greater than 600

0   500   1000 Miles

0   500   1000 Kilometers

Complete legend on page 5

ARCTIC DISTANCES

The shortest distance between some cities of the Northern Hemisphere is a great circle route across the Arctic.

4,300 Miles 7000 Kilometers

5,000 Miles 8100 Kilometers

to Chicago

Polar bears roam a vast, flat Arctic plain. The fur of the polar bear blends with the snowy white landscape.

CANADA

Lake Manitoba

Vancouver

Cape Flattery

Mt. Olympus 2428m

Grand Coulee Dam

Seattle

Franklin D. Roosevelt

WASHINGTON

Portland

Blue Mts.

Cape Blanco

OREGON

Columbia Plateau

Snake

MONTANA

Fort Peck Lake

Milk R.

Missouri R.

Lake Sakakawea

NORTH DAKOT

Coast Ranges

Cascade

Bitterroot Range

Salmon River

IDAHO

Mts.

American Falls Res.

Yellowstone

R O C K Y

Bighorn Mts.

Powder R.

Great

SOUT DAKO

Black Hills

Lake Oahe

Cape Mendocino

Sacramento Valley

Pyramid Lake

Goose Lake

Klamath

Humboldt R.

Carson Sink

NEVADA

Great Basin

Ruby Mts.

Great Salt Lake

Great Salt Lake Desert

Salmon River

Utah Lake

WYOMING

Pathfinder Res.

Wyoming Basin

Wasatch Range

Uinta Mts.

Seminoe Res.

W Y O M I N G

Front Range

Niobrara R.

Platte R.

S. Platte R.

Republican R.

NEBRAS

Platte R.

KA

San Francisco

Lake Tahoe

Sierra Nevada

UTAH

Sevier Lake

Green

M

COLORADO

Mt. Elbert 4399m

Denver

Pikes Peak 4301m

Smoky Hill

Arkansas R.

Monterey Bay

Coast Ranges

San Joaquin Valley

Mt. Whitney 418m

Death Valley -86m

CALIFORNIA

Colorado

Lake Powell

Lake Mead

Glen Canyon Dam

Grand Canyon

Colorado Plateau

Sangre de Cristo Mts.

Pt. Conception

Mojave Desert

Hoover Dam

OCEAN

Los Angeles

Channel Islands

Salton Sea

Imperial Valley

Parker Dam

ARIZONA

Phoenix

Salt R.

Gila R.

NEW MEXICO

Sacramento Mts.

Front Range

Canadian R.

N Canad

Llano Estacado

OK

Red R.

San Diego

Tijuana

Elephant Butte Res.

Rio Grande

El Paso

Pecos R.

TE

PACIFIC

Edwards Plateau

MEXICO

Monterrey

HAWAII inset:

160°W

158°W

156°W

Kauai

Niihau

Oahu

Molokai

Pearl Harbor

Lanai

Maui

Kahoolawe

PACIFIC OCEAN

Hawaii

Mauna Loa 4169m

HAWAII

0 100 200 Miles

0 100 200 Kilometers

ALASKA inset:

Point Barrow

Chukchi Sea

Beaufort Sea

70°W

RUSSIA

Brooks Range

ARCTIC CIRCLE

65°

Bering Strait

Seward Peninsula

ALASKA

CANADA

St. Lawrence I.

Norton Sound

Nunivak I.

Mt. McKinley 6194m

Range

60°

Anchorage

Bering Sea

Kenai Peninsula

Aleutian Islands

Alaska Peninsula

Kodiak I.

Gulf of Alaska

Alexander Archipelago

0 200 400 Miles

0 200 400 Kilometers

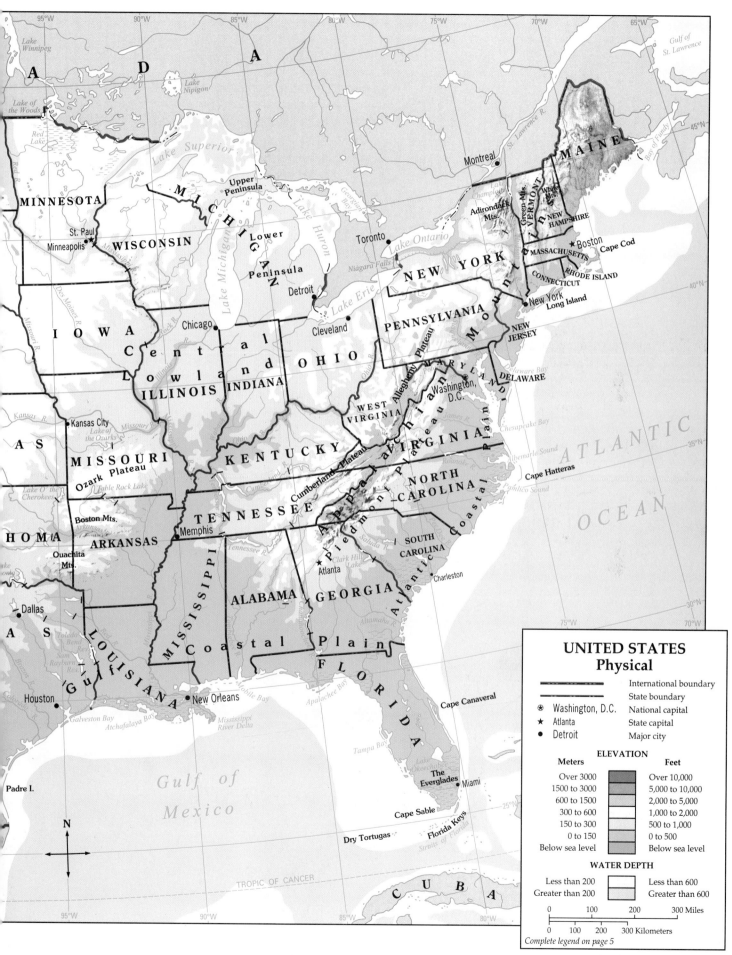

A N A D A

Lake Winnipeg

Lake of the Woods

Red Lake

Lake Nipigon

Lake Superior

Gulf of St. Lawrence

45°N

Montreal

MAINE

Bay of Fundy

MINNESOTA

MICHIGAN

Upper Peninsula

Lake Huron

Georgian Bay

Lake Champlain

Green Mts.
VERMONT

White Mts.
NEW HAMPSHIRE

St. Paul

Minneapolis

WISCONSIN

Lower Peninsula

Niagara Falls

Toronto

Lake Ontario

NEW YORK

Adirondack Mts.

★ Boston
MASSACHUSETTS Cape Cod

CONNECTICUT **RHODE ISLAND**

40°N

IOWA

Chicago

Detroit

Lake Erie

Cleveland

PENNSYLVANIA

New York
Long Island

NEW JERSEY

C e n t r a l

L o w l a n d

OHIO

Allegheny Plateau

MARYLAND

DELAWARE

Delaware Bay

Des Moines R.

Missouri R.

ILLINOIS **INDIANA**

Ohio R.

WEST VIRGINIA

Washington, D.C.

James R.

Chesapeake Bay

Kansas R.

Kansas City

Missouri R.

Lake of the Ozarks

KENTUCKY

Cumberland Plateau

VIRGINIA

Albemarle Sound

35°N

ATLANTIC

MISSOURI

Ozark Plateau

Table Rock Lake

Cumberland R.

A p p a l a c h i a n

NORTH CAROLINA

Cape Hatteras

Pamlico Sound

OCEAN

Lake O' the Cherokees

Boston Mts.

Arkansas R.

TENNESSEE

Tennessee R.

Piedmont Plateau

Roanoke R.

HOMA

Ouachita Mts.

Memphis

ARKANSAS

Clark Hill Lake

Saluda R.

SOUTH CAROLINA

A t l a n t i c

★ Atlanta

Charleston

ALABAMA

GEORGIA

C o a s t a l

30°N

Dallas

MISSISSIPPI

C o a s t a l   P l a i n

P l a i n

75°W

70°W

Altamaha R.

LOUISIANA

FLORIDA

Toledo Bend Res.

Sam Rayburn Res.

Gulf

Houston

New Orleans

Mobile Bay

Apalachee Bay

Cape Canaveral

Galveston Bay

Atchafalaya Bay

Mississippi River Delta

Padre I.

G u l f   o f

M e x i c o

Tampa Bay

Lake Okeechobee

The Everglades

Miami

25°N

Cape Sable

Florida Keys

Dry Tortugas

Straits of Florida

TROPIC OF CANCER

C U B A

95°W

90°W

85°W

80°W

UNITED STATES
Physical

⊛ Washington, D.C.	International boundary
	State boundary
	National capital
★ Atlanta	State capital
• Detroit	Major city

ELEVATION

Meters		Feet
Over 3000		Over 10,000
1500 to 3000		5,000 to 10,000
600 to 1500		2,000 to 5,000
300 to 600		1,000 to 2,000
150 to 300		500 to 1,000
0 to 150		0 to 500
Below sea level		Below sea level

WATER DEPTH

Less than 200		Less than 600
Greater than 200		Greater than 600

N

0   100   200   300 Miles

0 100 200 300 Kilometers

Complete legend on page 5

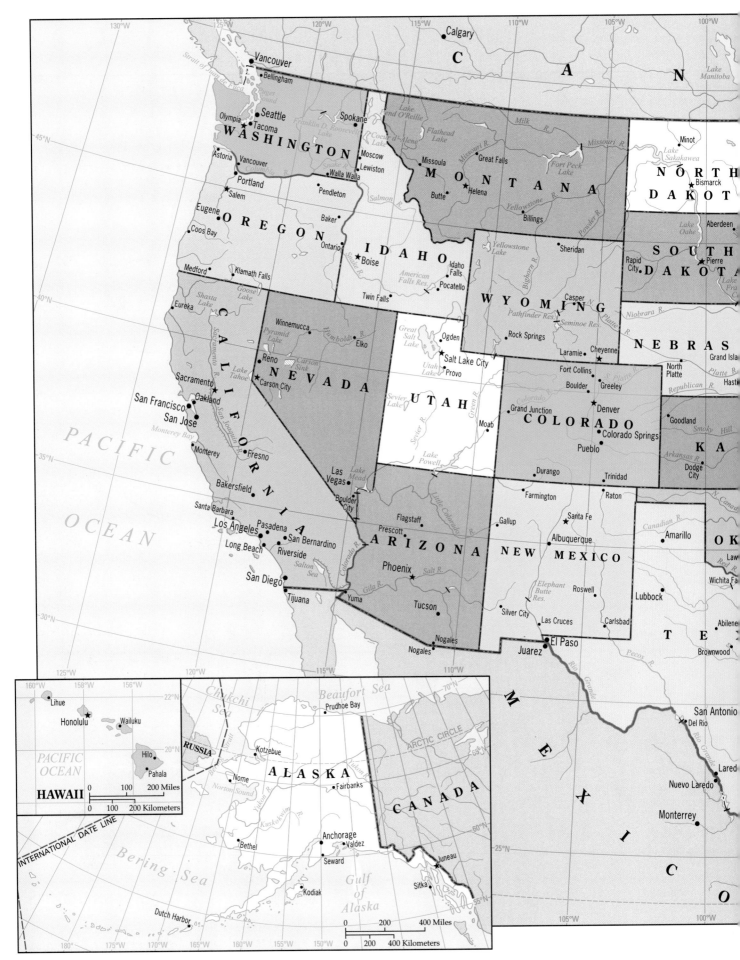

UNITED STATES
Political

BOUNDARIES

International boundary

State boundary

CITIES

● Chicago

• Anchorage

· Boulder

A city's relative size is shown by the size of its symbol and lettering.

⊗ Washington, D.C.   National capital

★ Honolulu   State capital

| 0 | 100 | 200 | 300 Miles |

| 0 | 100 | 200 | 300 Kilometers |

Complete legend on page 5

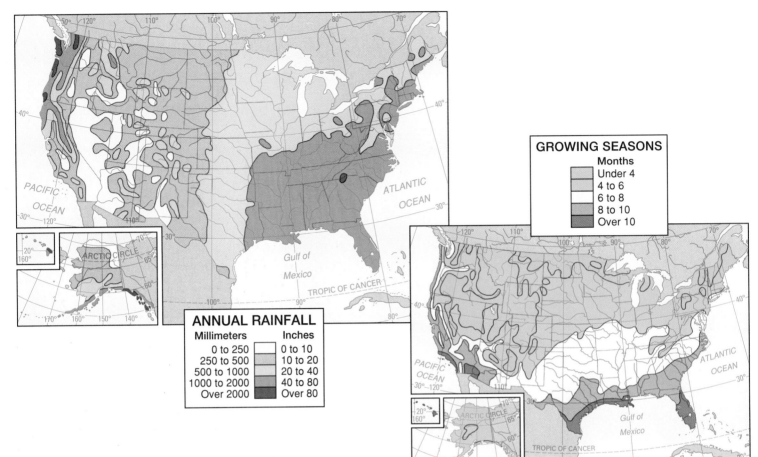

ANNUAL RAINFALL

Millimeters		Inches
0 to 250		0 to 10
250 to 500		10 to 20
500 to 1000		20 to 40
1000 to 2000		40 to 80
Over 2000		Over 80

GROWING SEASONS

Months
	Under 4
	4 to 6
	6 to 8
	8 to 10
	Over 10

Yosemite Falls, in California's Sierra Nevada, is one of the world's highest waterfalls.

ALASKA'S SIZE AND SHAPE

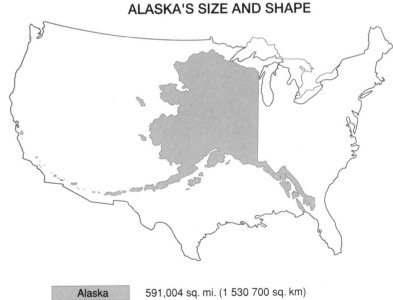

Alaska	591,004 sq. mi. (1 530 700 sq. km)
48 States	3,021,295 sq. mi. (7 825 112 sq. km)

Alaska is one-fifth the size of the first 48 states combined. It is twice as big as Texas, which is the second-largest state.

REGIONS OF THE UNITED STATES

Alaska

Pacific Northwest

Great Plains States

Great Lakes States

NORTHEAST

New England States

PACIFIC

ROCKY MOUNTAIN

MIDWEST

Middle Atlantic States

Hawaii

SOUTHWEST

SOUTHEAST

South Atlantic States

Gulf Coast States

States can be grouped into regions in many ways. This map identifies some traditional regions and regional names. It also shows that regions often overlap each other.

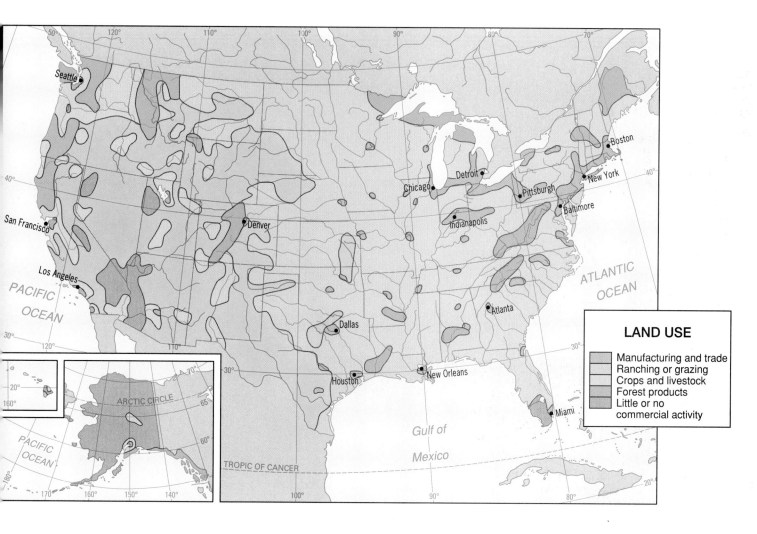

LAND USE

- Manufacturing and trade
- Ranching or grazing
- Crops and livestock
- Forest products
- Little or no commercial activity

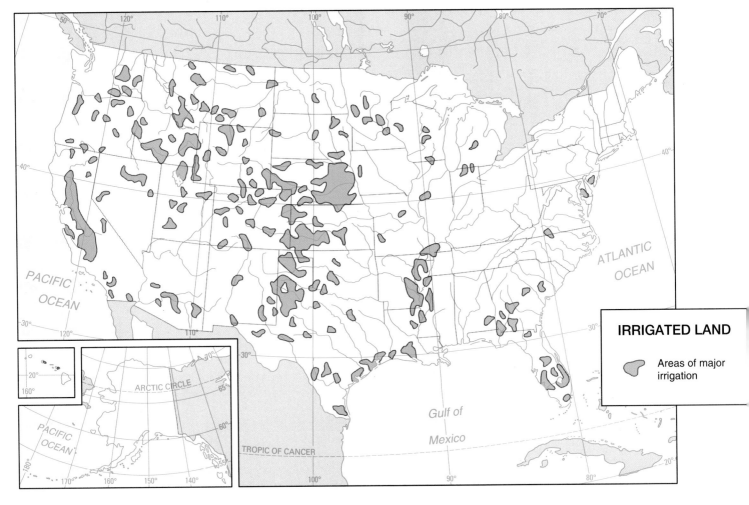

IRRIGATED LAND

Areas of major irrigation

Wheat fields on the Great Plains spread across vast areas. Farmers do not plant the same field every year, but alternate fields to conserve the soil.

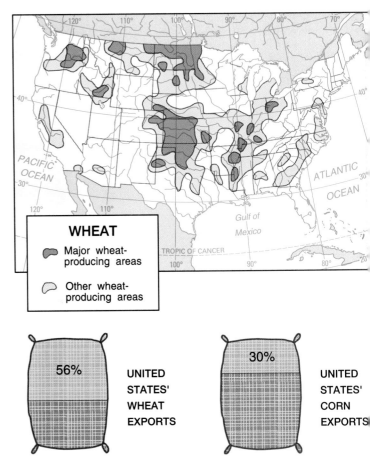

WHEAT

Major wheat-producing areas

Other wheat-producing areas

56% UNITED STATES' WHEAT EXPORTS

30% UNITED STATES' CORN EXPORTS

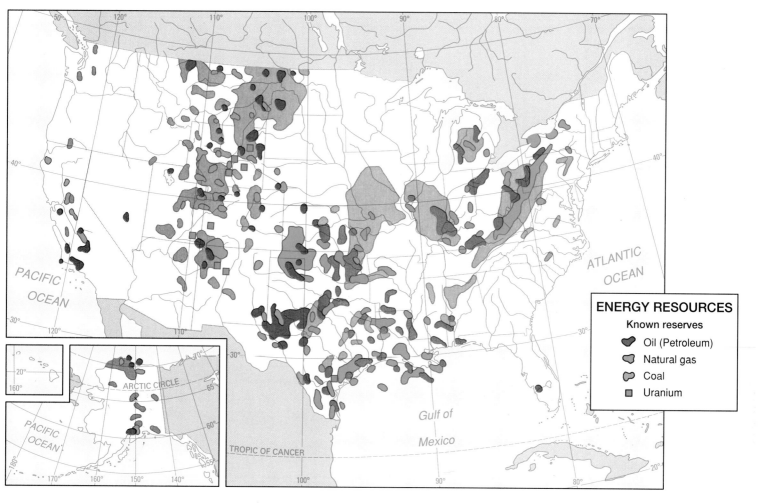

ENERGY RESOURCES
Known reserves

- Oil (Petroleum)
- Natural gas
- Coal
- Uranium

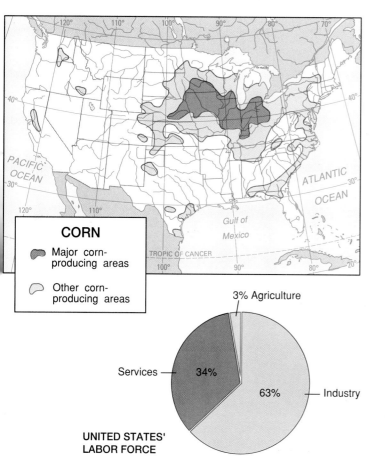

CORN

- Major corn-producing areas
- Other corn-producing areas

3% Agriculture

Services 34%

63% Industry

UNITED STATES' LABOR FORCE

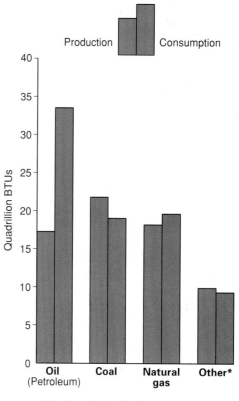

ANNUAL U.S. ENERGY PRODUCTION AND CONSUMPTION

Production   Consumption

Quadrillion BTUs

Oil (Petroleum)   Coal   Natural gas   Other*

*Nuclear, hydroelectric, geothermal

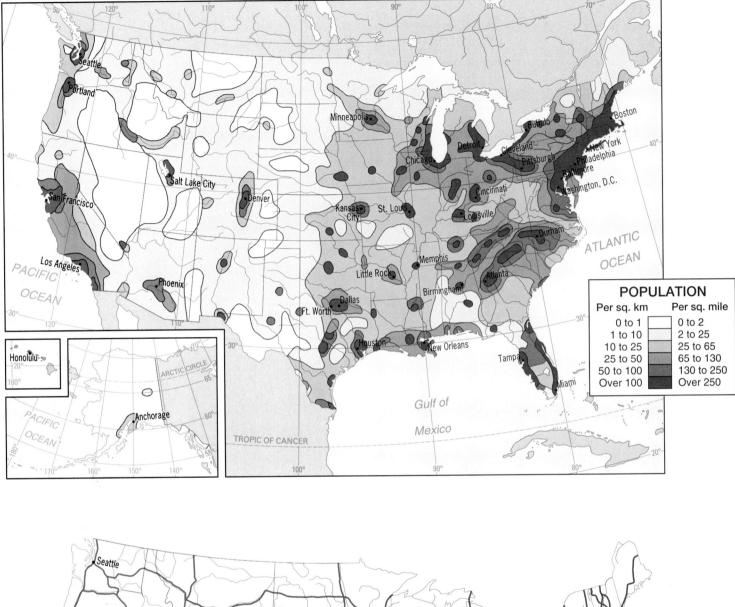

POPULATION

Per sq. km	Per sq. mile
0 to 1	0 to 2
1 to 10	2 to 25
10 to 25	25 to 65
25 to 50	65 to 130
50 to 100	130 to 250
Over 100	Over 250

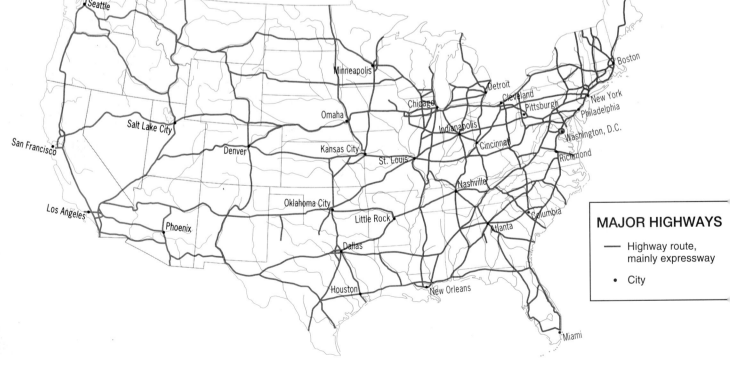

MAJOR HIGHWAYS

— Highway route, mainly expressway

• City

CITIES OF THE UNITED STATES

In 1790 only 5 percent of the nation's people lived in cities. Since then the population has steadily become more and more urban. Americans continue to move away from the country's rural areas, which are defined by the Census Bureau as communities with fewer than 2,500 people.

The most rapid growth in recent years has been in the suburbs outside the big cities. But the cities remain centers of the nation's business and cultural life.

74% URBAN

U.S. URBAN POPULATION

New York is the largest city in the United States and one of the oldest. Restricted by its location, it can only grow upward, not outward.

Chicago is the transportation crossroads of the United States. The city's long history as a leading transportation center has made it an important center of commerce too.

Los Angeles has a central business district ringed by freeways. Like most cities, it is dependent on trucks and automobiles.

Miami is in the Sun Belt, which extends through the Southeast, Southwest, and some Pacific states. Partly because of their climate, most Sun Belt cities are growing rapidly.

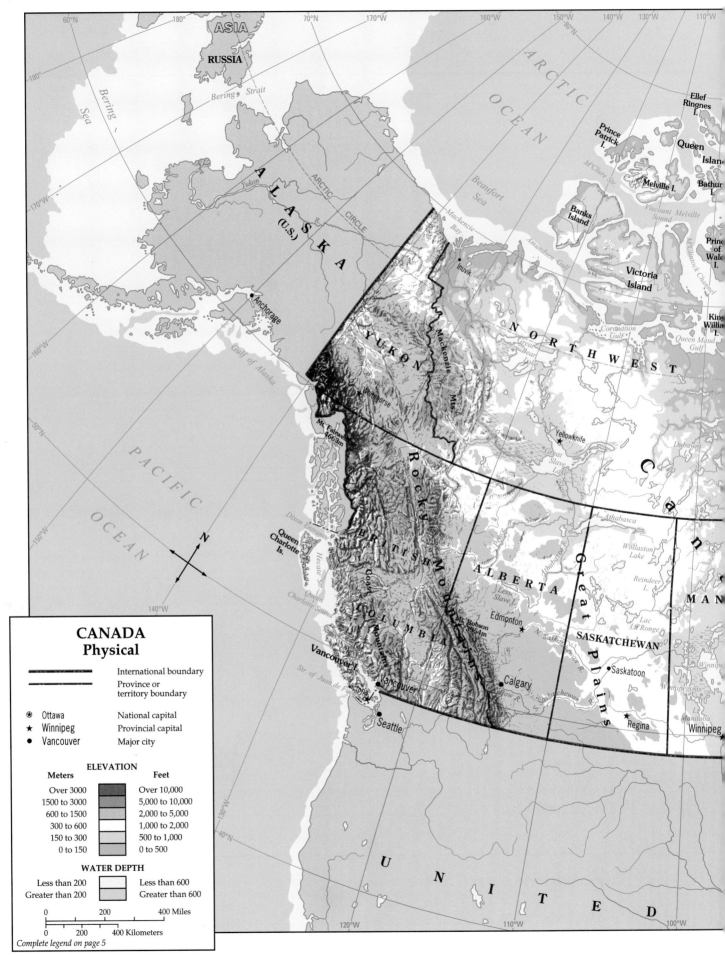

CANADA
Physical

————	International boundary
————	Province or territory boundary
⊗ Ottawa	National capital
★ Winnipeg	Provincial capital
● Vancouver	Major city

ELEVATION

Meters		Feet
Over 3000		Over 10,000
1500 to 3000		5,000 to 10,000
600 to 1500		2,000 to 5,000
300 to 600		1,000 to 2,000
150 to 300		500 to 1,000
0 to 150		0 to 500

WATER DEPTH

Less than 200		Less than 600
Greater than 200		Greater than 600

0   200   400 Miles
0   200   400 Kilometers

Complete legend on page 5

GREENLAND
(KALAALLIT NUNAAT) (Denmark)

ICELAND

ATLANTIC

OCEAN

Denmark Strait

ARCTIC CIRCLE

Cape Farewell

80°N

70°N

60°N

10°N

20°W

30°W

40°W

Axel
Heiberg
I.

Ellesmere Island

zabeth

Kane
Basin

Devon Island

Baffin
Bay

Lancaster Sound

Somerset
I.

Gulf of Boothia

othia
Pen.

Baffin
Island

Melville
Peninsula

Foxe
Basin

Foxe
Channel

Cumberland Sd.

Iqaluit

Frobisher Bay

T E R R I T O R I E S

Foxe
Peninsula

Southampton
I.

Chesterfield
Inlet

Coats
I.

Mansel
I.

Ungava
Peninsula

Ungava
Bay

Torngat Mts.

Cape
Chidley

Labrador
Sea

50°N

Hudson
Strait

Hudson

Bay

James
Bay

Belcher
Is.

Labrador

Happy Valley-
Goose Bay

Churchill R.

NEWFOUNDLAND

Newfoundland

St. John's

Cape Race

40°W

50°N

OBA

C a n a d i a n

S h i e l d

L.
Mistassini

QUEBEC

Albany R.

ONTARIO

Lake of
the Woods

Thunder
Bay

Superior

L. Superior

Nipigon

Sault Ste.
Marie

L. Nipissing

Georgian Bay

L. Huron

L. Michigan

Detroit

Windsor

L. Erie

Niagara
Falls

Toronto

L. Ontario

L.
Simcoe

Ottawa

Montreal

Québec

St. Lawrence R.

Gaspé Pen.

NEW
BRUNSWICK

Fredericton

Bay of Fundy

Gulf of
St. Lawrence

Anticosti
I.

Strait of Belle Isle

PRINCE
EDWARD
ISLAND

NOVA

SCOTIA

Halifax

Cape Sable

Cape
Breton
Island

Sable I.

Miquelon
(Fr.)

St. Pierre
(Fr.)

Newfoundland

ATLANTIC

OCEAN

40°N

50°N

S T A T E S

90°W

80°W

70°W

60°N

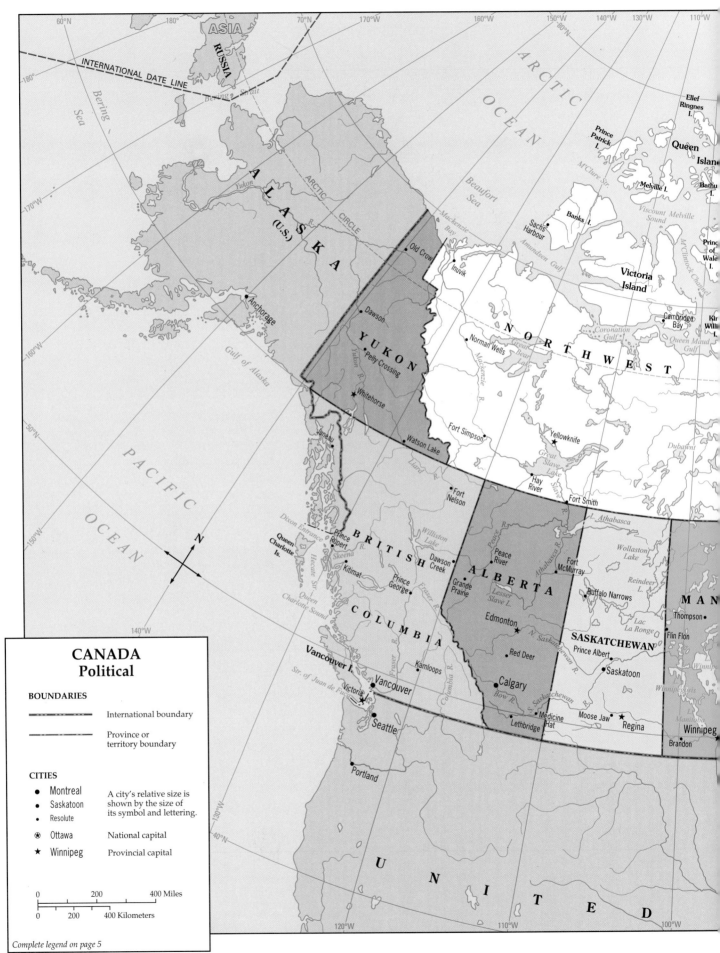

**CANADA
Political**

BOUNDARIES

- - - - International boundary

—— Province or
territory boundary

CITIES

● Montreal   A city's relative size is
● Saskatoon   shown by the size of
● Resolute   its symbol and lettering.

⊛ Ottawa   National capital

★ Winnipeg   Provincial capital

0   200   400 Miles
0   200   400 Kilometers

Complete legend on page 5

G R E E N L A N D
(KALAALLIT NUNAAT) (Denmark)

ICELAND

ARCTIC CIRCLE

Denmark Strait

ATLANTIC

OCEAN

Axel
Heiberg
I.

Ellesmere

Island

Kane
Basin

Elizabeth

Devon I.

Resolute

merset I.

Lancaster Sound

Baffin

Bay

Clyde

Baffin
Island

Gulf
of
Boothia

Godthab

Davis
Strait

Cape Farewell

Pelly Bay

Foxe
Basin

Cumberland Sd.

Iqaluit

Frobisher Bay

T E R R I T O R I E S

Chesterfield
Inlet

Southampton
I.

Foxe Channel

Labrador

Sea

Coats I.

Mansel I.

Hudson

Strait

Salluit

Ungava
Bay

Churchill

Hudson

Bay

Belcher
Is.

Kuujjuarapik

Kuujjuaq

Feuilles

George R.

Smallwood
Res.

Happy Valley
Goose Bay

NEWFOUNDLAND

Churchill R.

OBA

Severn R.

Fort Severn

James
Bay

Labrador
City

Newfoundland

St. John's

Winisk R.

Albany R.

Moosonee

Manicouagan
Lake

Corner
Brook

Kenora

ONTARIO

L.
Nipigon

L.
Mistassini

QUEBEC

Sept-Îles

Anticosti
I.

Newfoundland

ST. PIERRE AND
MIQUELON
(France)

Lake
of
the Woods

Thunder
Bay

L. Superior

Sault Ste.
Marie

Sudbury

L.
Nipissing

St. Lawrence R.

Gulf
of
St. Lawrence

PRINCE
EDWARD
ISLAND

Charlottetown

Cape Breton I.

Minneapolis

L. Michigan

L. Huron

Georgian
Bay

Val-d'Or

Hull

Ottawa

Quebec

Montreal

John R.

NEW
BRUNSWICK

Fredericton

NOVA
SCOTIA

Halifax

Sable I.
(Nova Scotia)

L. Simcoe

Kingston

Saint John

Bay of Fundy

Chicago

Detroit

Windsor

London

Hamilton

Toronto

L. Ontario

Buffalo

Niagara
Falls

L. Erie

Boston

Yarmouth

New York

ATLANTIC

OCEAN

S T A T E S

90°W 80°W 70°W 60°W

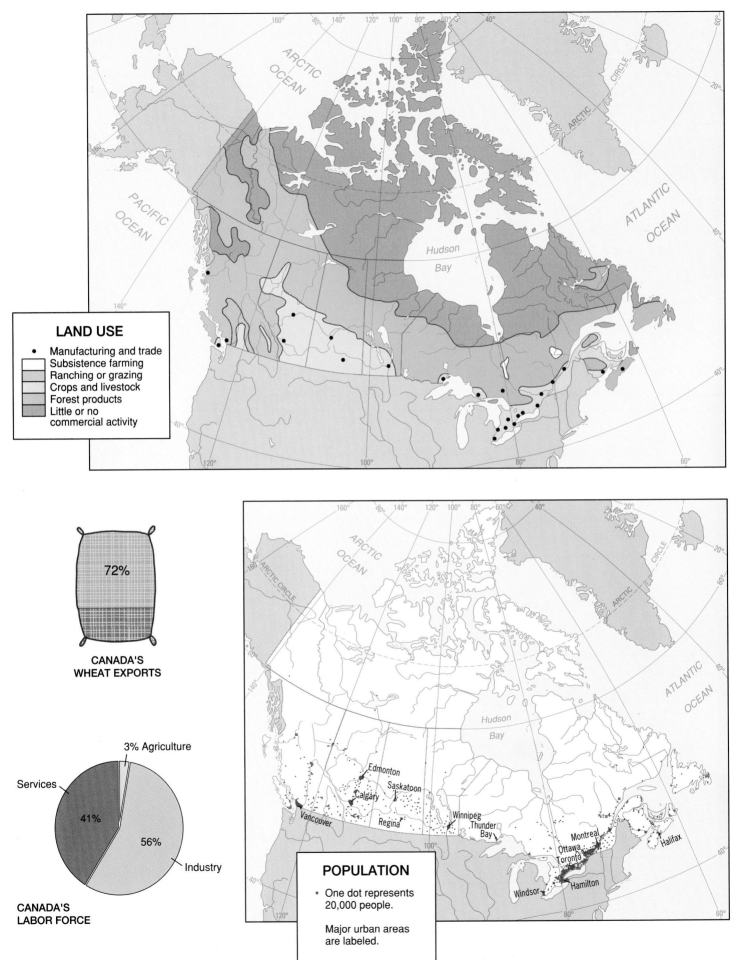

LAND USE

- Manufacturing and trade
- Subsistence farming
- Ranching or grazing
- Crops and livestock
- Forest products
- Little or no commercial activity

CANADA'S WHEAT EXPORTS

72%

CANADA'S LABOR FORCE

Services 41%
Industry 56%
3% Agriculture

POPULATION

- One dot represents 20,000 people.

Major urban areas are labeled.

Edmonton
Saskatoon
Calgary
Vancouver
Regina
Winnipeg
Thunder Bay
Montreal
Ottawa
Toronto
Halifax
Hamilton
Windsor

Millions of trees are harvested from Canada's vast forests each year. Waterways and trucks carry the logs away for shipment to the United States or overseas. Canada is a leading exporter of forest products.

CANADA'S FORESTRY EXPORTS

EXPORT PRODUCTS

Forestry leads to the manufacture of many Canadian products. Pulp, newsprint, and lumber are the greatest uses of harvested wood.

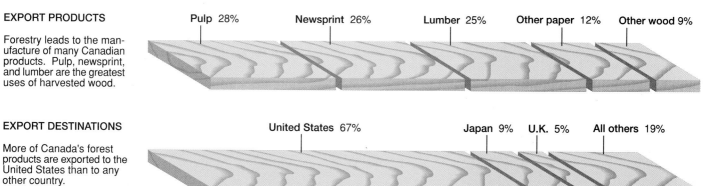

Pulp 28% Newsprint 26% Lumber 25% Other paper 12% Other wood 9%

EXPORT DESTINATIONS

More of Canada's forest products are exported to the United States than to any other country.

United States 67% Japan 9% U.K. 5% All others 19%

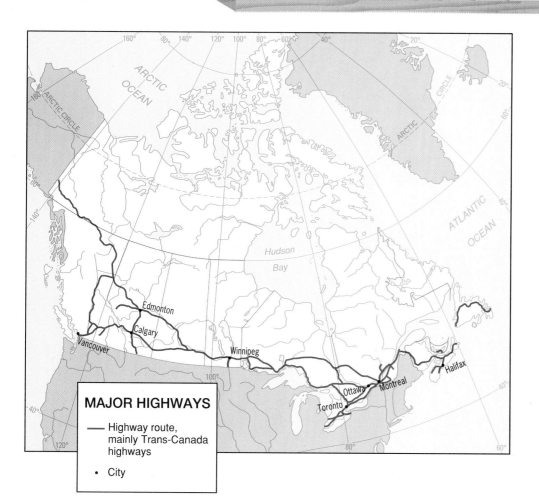

MAJOR HIGHWAYS

— Highway route, mainly Trans-Canada highways

• City

MINERAL RESOURCES

Of Canada's many mineral resources, iron ore is mined in the greatest quantity. It totals more than 15 times the weight of the others combined.

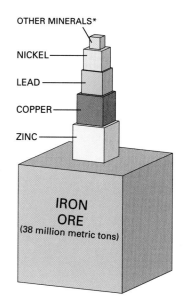

OTHER MINERALS*

NICKEL

LEAD

COPPER

ZINC

IRON ORE
(38 million metric tons)

*Molybdenum, Uranium, Silver, Gold

Los Angeles

UNITED STATES

NORTH AMERICA

Colorado R.

–30°N

Guadalupe I.

Angel de la Guardia I.

Gulf (Sea) of California (Cortez)

Rio Grande

Amistad Res.

GULF OF

New Orleans

Cedros I.

Sebastián Vizcaíno Bay

Tiburon I.

Conchos R.

Houston

Cape Eugenia

TROPIC OF CANCER

Santa Margarita I.

San Jose I.

Sierra Madre Occidental

Plateau of Mexico

MEXICO

Monterrey

Madre Lagoon

MEXICO

Cape San Lucas

Sierra Madre Oriental

–20°N

Tres Marias Is.

Cape Corrientes

Chapala

Cape Rojo

Revillagigedo Is.

PACIFIC

Balsas R.

Paricutin Volcano 2808m

Mexico City

Orizaba 5700m

Bay of Campeche

Yucatan

Popocatepetl Volcano 5452m

Miguel Aleman Res.

Términos Lagoon

Peninsula

OCEAN

Acapulco

Sierra Madre del Sur

Isthmus of Tehuantepec

Grijalva R.

BELI

110°W

Gulf of Tehuantepec

El Chicon 1060m

GUATEMALA

Tajumulco 4211m

Central

Guatemala City

Gulf of Fonsec

EL SALVADOR

N

–10°N

MIDDLE AMERICA
Physical

——————		International boundary
⊛	Havana	National capital
●	Monterrey	Major city

ELEVATION

Meters		Feet
Over 3000		Over 10,000
1500 to 3000		5,000 to 10,000
600 to 1500		2,000 to 5,000
300 to 600		1,000 to 2,000
150 to 300		500 to 1,000
0 to 150		0 to 500

WATER DEPTH

Less than 200		Less than 600
Greater than 200		Greater than 600

| 0 | 100 | 200 | 300 | 400 Miles |

| 0 | 100 | 200 | 300 | 400 Kilometers |

Complete legend on page 5

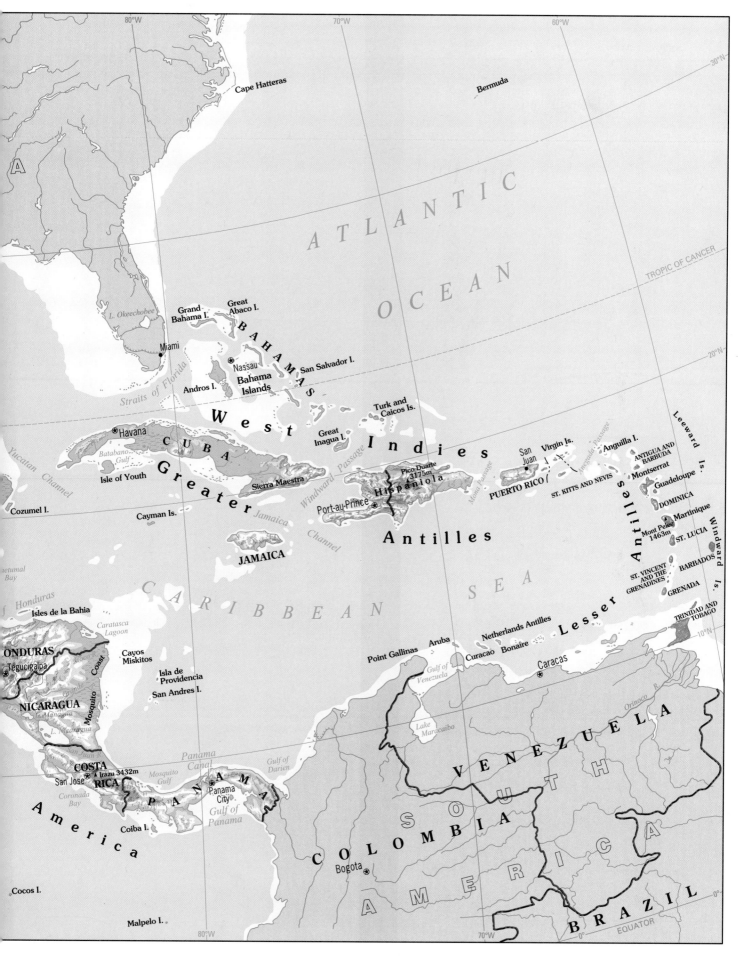

Cape Hatteras

Bermuda

A T L A N T I C

O C E A N

TROPIC OF CANCER

L. Okeechobee

Grand
Bahama I.

Great
Abaco I.

Miami

BAHAMAS

Nassau

San Salvador I.

20°N

Andros I.

Bahama
Islands

Straits of Florida

W e s t

Turk and
Caicos Is.

Yucatan Channel

Havana

CUBA

Batabano
Gulf

Isle of Youth

Sierra Maestra

Great
Inagua I.

I n d i e s

San
Juan

Virgin Is.

Anguilla I.

Leeward Is.

ANTIGUA AND
BARBUDA

Cozumel I.

G r e a t e r

Windward Passage

Hispaniola

Pico Duarte
3175m

Mona Passage

Montserrat

Guadeloupe

PUERTO RICO

ST. KITTS AND NEVIS

DOMINICA

Cayman Is.

Jamaica

Port-au-Prince

Mont Pelee
1463m

Martinique

ST. LUCIA

Windward Is.

actumal
Bay

Channel

A n t i l l e s

Lesser Antilles

JAMAICA

ST. VINCENT
AND THE
GRENADINES

BARBADOS

GRENADA

f Honduras

C A R I B B E A N

S E A

TRINIDAD AND
TOBAGO

Isles de la Bahia

Caratasca
Lagoon

Netherlands Antilles

10°N

ONDURAS

Tegucigalpa

Cayos
Miskitos

Point Gallinas

Aruba

Curacao Bonaire

Caracas

Gulf of
Venezuela

Isla de
Providencia

San Andres I.

NICARAGUA

Managua

Mosquito Coast

L. Nicaragua

Gulf of
Darien

Lake
Maracaibo

V E N E Z U E L A

Orinoco

Grande

COSTA

Panama
Canal

San Jose

RICA

Irazu 3432m

Mosquito
Gulf

Panama
City

Gulf of
Darien

S

O

U

T

H

COLOMBIA

Coronada
Bay

P A N A M A

Gulf of
Panama

A

M

E

R

I

C

A

America

Coiba I.

Bogota

Cocos I.

Malpelo I.

B R A Z I L

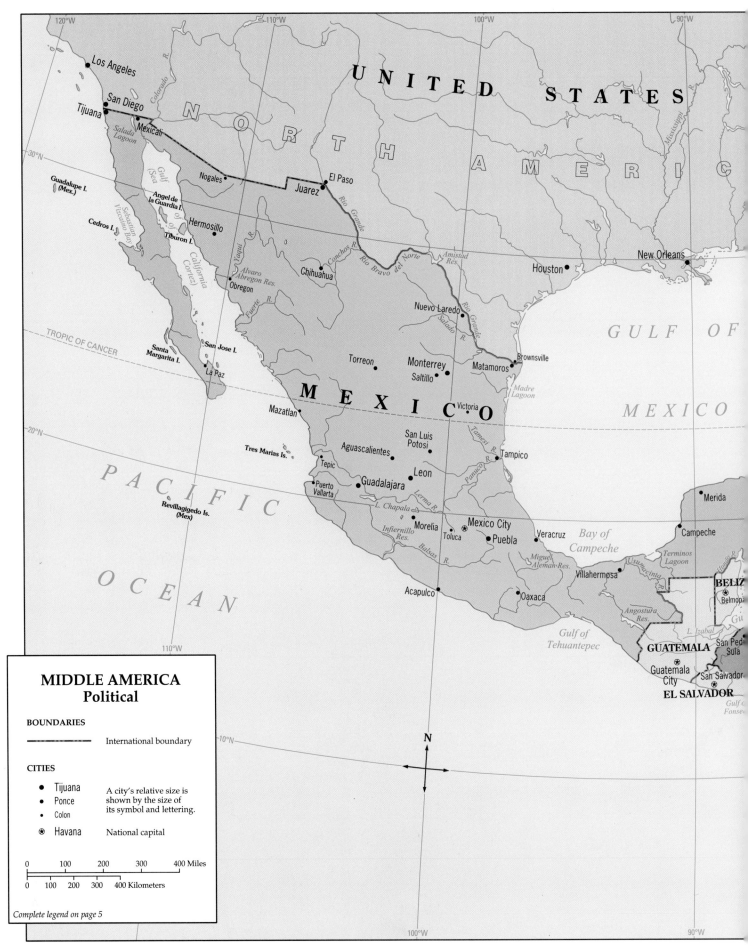

UNITED STATES

NORTH AMERICA

Los Angeles
San Diego
Tijuana
Mexicali
Nogales
El Paso
Juarez
New Orleans
Houston

Guadalupe I.
(Mex.)
Angel de
la Guardia I.
Hermosillo
Cedros I.
Sebastian
Vizcaino Bay
Tiburon I.
Chihuahua

Salada
Lagoon
Gulf
(Sea)
California
(Cortez)
Yaqui R.
Alvaro
Abregon Res.
Obregon
Fuerte R.
Conchos R.
Rio Grande
Rio Bravo del Norte
Amistad
Res.
Nuevo Laredo
Rio Grande
Salado R.
Brownsville
Matamoros

TROPIC OF CANCER

Santa
Margarita I.
San Jose I.
La Paz
Torreon
Monterrey
Saltillo
Madre
Lagoon
GULF OF
MEXICO

M E X I C O
Victoria

Mazatlan
San Luis
Potosi
Tamesi R.
Tampico

Tres Marias Is.
Aguascalientes
Leon
Ponuco R.

PACIFIC
Tepic
Guadalajara
Lerma R.
Revillagigedo Is.
(Mex.)
Puerto
Vallarta
L. Chapala
Infiernillo
Res.
Morelia
Toluca
Mexico City
Puebla
Veracruz
Bay of
Campeche
Merida

OCEAN
Balsas R.
Miguel
Aleman Res.
Villahermosa
Usumacinta R.
Terminos
Lagoon
Campeche
BELIZ

Acapulco
Oaxaca
Gulf of
Tehuantepec
Angostura
Res.
L. Izabal
Belmopa
GUATEMALA
San Ped
Sula
Guatemala
City
San Salvador
EL SALVADOR
Gulf o
Fonse

N

MIDDLE AMERICA
Political

BOUNDARIES

—————————— International boundary

CITIES

● Tijuana   A city's relative size is
● Ponce   shown by the size of
· Colon   its symbol and lettering.

⊛ Havana   National capital

0   100   200   300   400 Miles

0 100 200 300 400 Kilometers

Complete legend on page 5

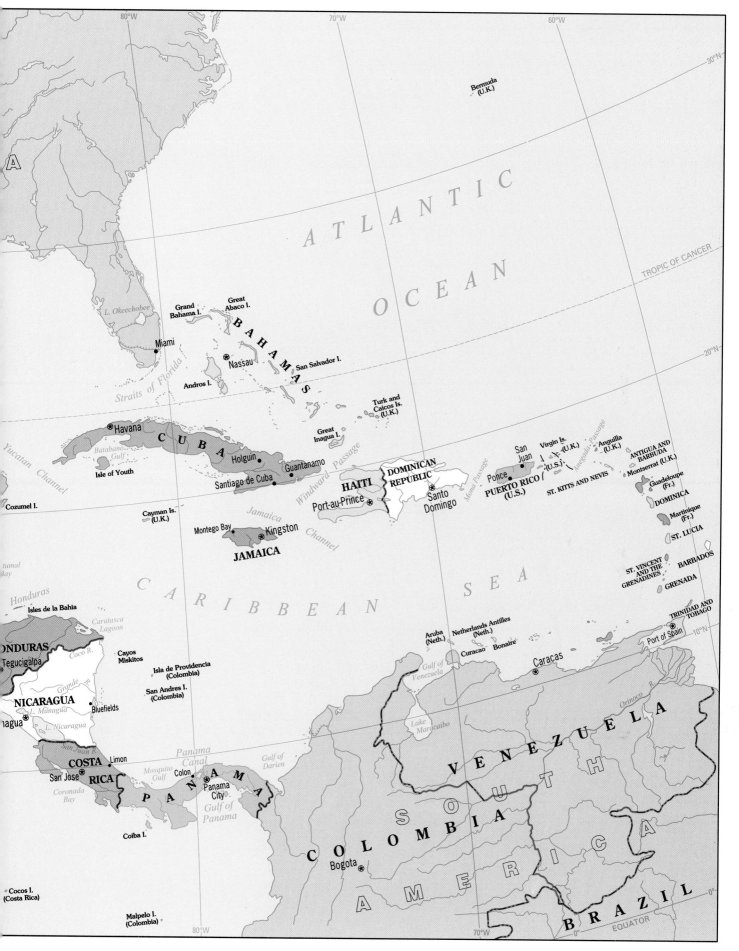

ATLANTIC

OCEAN

TROPIC OF CANCER

30°N

80°W
70°W
60°W

Bermuda
(U.K.)

20°N

L. Okeechobee

Grand
Bahama I.

Great
Abaco I.

Miami

B A H A M A S

Nassau

San Salvador I.

Andros I.

Straits of Florida

Turk and
Caicos Is.
(U.K.)

Great
Inagua I.

Havana

C U B A

Batabano
Gulf

Holguin

Yucatan Channel

Isle of Youth

Santiago de Cuba

Guantanamo

Windward Passage

DOMINICAN
REPUBLIC

HAITI

Mona Passage

San
Juan

Virgin Is.

(U.K.)

(U.S.)

Anguilla
(U.K.)

ANTIGUA AND
BARBUDA

Cozumel I.

Cayman Is.
(U.K.)

Jamaica

Montego Bay

Kingston

Jamaica
Channel

Port-au-Prince

Santo
Domingo

Ponce

PUERTO RICO
(U.S.)

ST. KITTS AND NEVIS

Montserrat (U.K.)

Guadeloupe
(Fr.)

DOMINICA

Martinique
(Fr.)

ST. LUCIA

JAMAICA

C A R I B B E A N

S E A

ST. VINCENT
AND THE
GRENADINES

BARBADOS

GRENADA

Honduras

Isles de la Bahia

Caratasca
Lagoon

ONDURAS

Coco R.

Tegucigalpa

tumal
Bay

Cayos
Miskitos

Isla de Providencia
(Colombia)

San Andres I.
(Colombia)

Aruba
(Neth.)

Netherlands Antilles
(Neth.)

Curacao

Bonaire

Caracas

TRINIDAD AND
TOBAGO

Port of Spain

10°N

Gulf of
Venezuela

NICARAGUA

L. Managua

Bluefields

agua

L. Nicaragua

Lake
Maracaibo

V E N E Z U E L A

San Juan R.

Panama
Canal

Gulf of
Darien

Orinoco R.

COSTA

Limon

Mosquito
Gulf

Colon

S O U T H

San Jose

RICA

P A N A M A

Panama
City

Coronada
Bay

Gulf of
Panama

C O L O M B I A

Coiba I.

A M E R I C A

Bogota

Cocos I.
(Costa Rica)

B R A Z I L

Malpelo I.
(Colombia)

80°W

70°W

0°

EQUATOR

0°

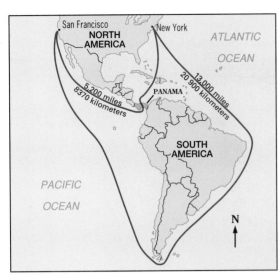

PANAMA CANAL

The Panama Canal cuts through the Isthmus of Panama to connect the Atlantic and Pacific Oceans. Ships save thousands of miles and several days by using the canal to travel between Atlantic and Pacific ports.

France began building the canal in 1878, and the Unites States completed it in 1914. In 1977, the United States and Panama signed a treaty giving Panama control of the waterway in 1999.

Because of its narrowness, the canal is a potential "choke point." If it were blocked or destroyed, shipping between the two oceans would be seriously disrupted.

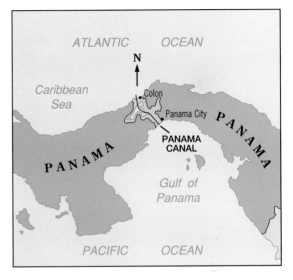

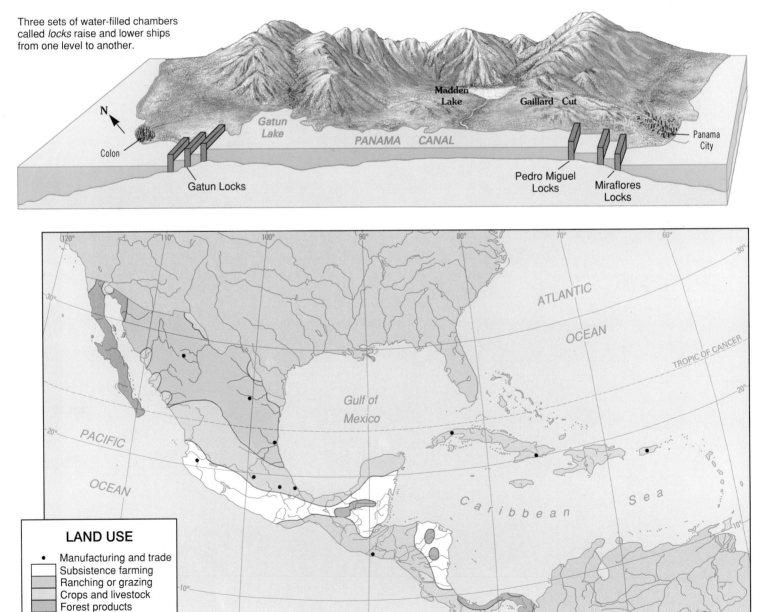

Three sets of water-filled chambers called *locks* raise and lower ships from one level to another.

LAND USE
- Manufacturing and trade
- Subsistence farming
- Ranching or grazing
- Crops and livestock
- Forest products
- Little or no commercial activity

Mexico City is one of the largest urban areas in the world.
Polluted air is frequently trapped above it by surrounding mountains.

GROWTH OF LARGE URBAN AREAS: Population in millions

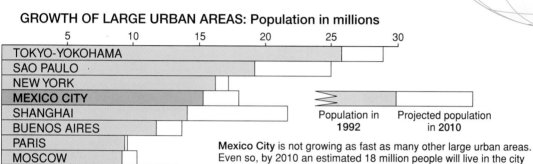

	5	10	15	20	25	30
TOKYO-YOKOHAMA						
SAO PAULO						
NEW YORK						
MEXICO CITY						
SHANGHAI						
BUENOS AIRES						
PARIS						
MOSCOW						
CAIRO						
KARACHI						

Population in 1992   Projected population in 2010

Mexico City is not growing as fast as many other large urban areas. Even so, by 2010 an estimated 18 million people will live in the city and its suburbs, more than in any other city in North America.

Middle America is part of a larger culture region called Latin America, which includes 33 countries. Most of the people in this region speak one of the Latin-based languages of Spanish, Portuguese, or French.

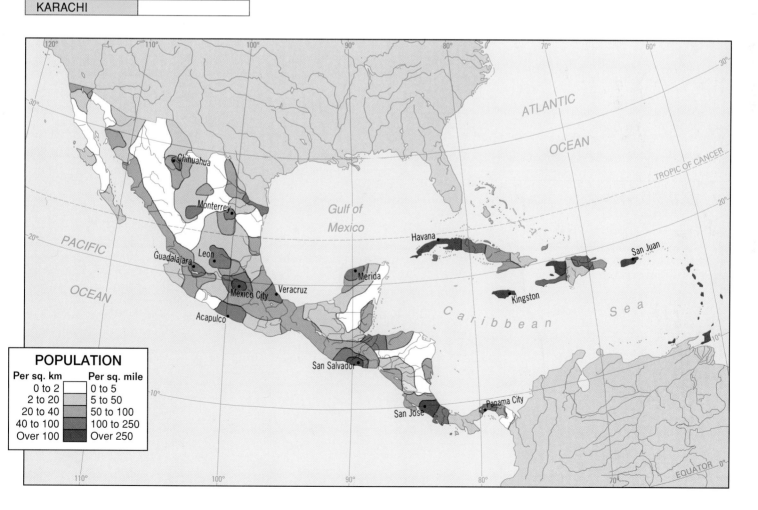

POPULATION

Per sq. km	Per sq. mile
0 to 2	0 to 5
2 to 20	5 to 50
20 to 40	50 to 100
40 to 100	100 to 250
Over 100	Over 250

West Indies

Havana⊛
CUBA
Greater
Antilles
Jamaica
Hispaniola
HAITI DOM. REP.
Puerto Rico
Lesser
Antilles

MEXICO
BELIZE
GUATEMALA
HONDURAS
EL SALVADOR
NICARAGUA
Lake Nicaragua
COSTA RICA
PANAMA
Isthmus of Panama
Gulf of Panama

CARIBBEAN SEA

ATLANTIC OCEAN

Pt. Gallinas
Curacao
Caracas⊛
Trinidad

Cocos I.
Malpelo I.

VENEZUELA
Llanos
Bogota⊛
COLOMBIA
Cordillera
Oriental

Georgetown
Paramaribo⊛
GUYANA
Cayenne
Mt. Roraima 2772m
SURINAME FR. GUIANA
Guiana Highlands

Orinoco
Lake Maracaibo
Angel Falls
Guaviare
Negro

Mouths of the Amazon River
Marajo I.

Quito⊛
ECUADOR
Mt. Chimborazo 6267m
Gulf of Guayaquil
Pt. Parinas
Pt. Aguja

EQUATOR

Amazon Basin

BRAZIL

Galapagos Islands

Fernando de Noronha
Pt. Calcanhar

Maranon
Juru
Amazon
Purus R.
Madeira R.
Tapajos R.
Xingu R.
Tocantins R.
Parnaiba R.

P E R U

Andes

Mt. Huascaran 6768m

Lima⊛

Mato Grosso Plateau

Brazilian Highlands

Brasilia⊛

Paulo Afonso Falls
Recife

La Paz⊛
Mt. Sajam 6542m
BOLIVIA
Sucre⊛
Lake Poopo

Gran Chaco
PARAGUAY
Asuncion⊛

Sierra Espinhaco
Sao Francisco R.
Tres Marias Res.
Campos
Furnas Res.

Agulhas Negras 2787m
Cape Frio
Rio de Janiero
Trindade

PACIFIC OCEAN

San Felix I.
San Ambrosio I.

Atacama Desert
Ojos del Salado 6880m
Salado

Parana R.
Iguacu Falls
Uruguay R.

Great Escarpment

TROPIC OF CAPRICORN

N

Juan Fernandez Islands

Santiago⊛
Aconcagua 6960m
Colorado R.
Pampas
ARGENTINA
Buenos Aires
URUGUAY
Montevideo⊛
Rio de la Plata
Cape San Antonio

Patos Lagoon
Mirim L.

ATLANTIC OCEAN

Negro R.
Blanca Bay

Chiloe I.
Chonos Archipelago
Gulf of San Jorge

Gulf of San Matias
Valdes Peninsula
Patagonia

Cape Tres Puntas

Wellington I.
Queen Adelaide Archipelago
Punta Arenas
Strait of Magellan
Tierra del Fuego
Cape Horn

Falkland Is. (Islas Malvinas)

Scotia Sea

South Georgia I.

Drake Passage

SOUTH AMERICA
Physical

—————— International boundary
⊛ Lima National capital
● Recife Major city

ELEVATION

Meters		Feet
Over 6000		Over 20,000
3000 to 6000		10,000 to 20,000
1500 to 3000		5,000 to 10,000
600 to 1500		2,000 to 5,000
300 to 600		1,000 to 2,000
150 to 300		500 to 1,000
0 to 150		0 to 500

WATER DEPTH

Less than 200		Less than 600
Greater than 200		Greater than 600

0 250 500 750 1000 Miles
0 250 500 1000 Kilometers

Complete legend on page 5

SOUTH AMERICA
Political

BOUNDARIES

——————— International boundary

CITIES

● Sao Paulo
● Fortaleza
· Cuzco

A city's relative size is shown by the size of its symbol and lettering.

⊛ Lima   National capital

| 0 | 250 | 500 | 750 | 1000 Miles |

| 0 | 250 | 500 | 750 | 1000 Kilometers |

Complete legend on page 5

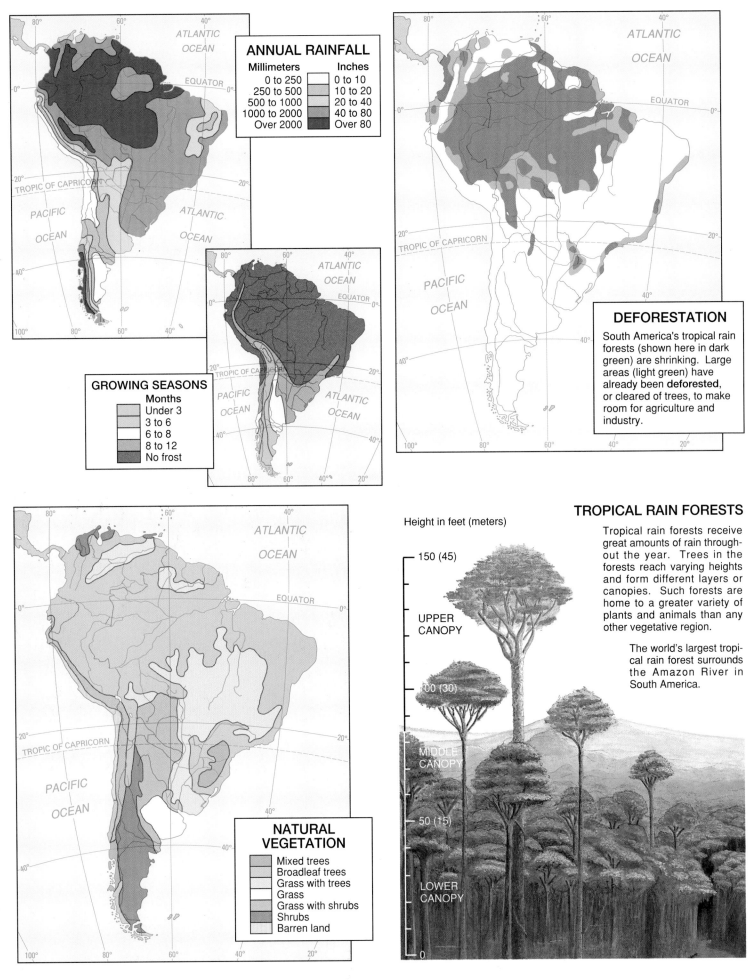

ANNUAL RAINFALL

Millimeters		Inches
0 to 250		0 to 10
250 to 500		10 to 20
500 to 1000		20 to 40
1000 to 2000		40 to 80
Over 2000		Over 80

GROWING SEASONS

Months
- Under 3
- 3 to 6
- 6 to 8
- 8 to 12
- No frost

DEFORESTATION

South America's tropical rain forests (shown here in dark green) are shrinking. Large areas (light green) have already been **deforested**, or cleared of trees, to make room for agriculture and industry.

NATURAL VEGETATION

- Mixed trees
- Broadleaf trees
- Grass with trees
- Grass
- Grass with shrubs
- Shrubs
- Barren land

TROPICAL RAIN FORESTS

Tropical rain forests receive great amounts of rain throughout the year. Trees in the forests reach varying heights and form different layers or canopies. Such forests are home to a greater variety of plants and animals than any other vegetative region.

The world's largest tropical rain forest surrounds the Amazon River in South America.

Height in feet (meters)

150 (45)

UPPER CANOPY

100 (30)

MIDDLE CANOPY

50 (15)

LOWER CANOPY

0

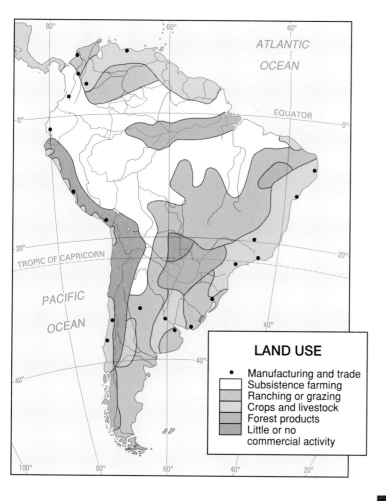

LAND USE

- • Manufacturing and trade
- Subsistence farming
- Ranching or grazing
- Crops and livestock
- Forest products
- Little or no commercial activity

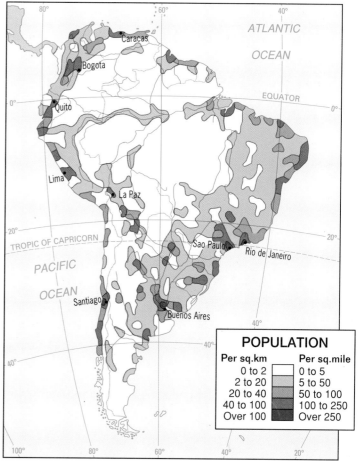

POPULATION

Per sq.km	Per sq.mile
0 to 2	0 to 5
2 to 20	5 to 50
20 to 40	50 to 100
40 to 100	100 to 250
Over 100	Over 250

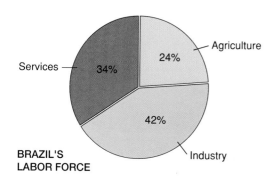

BRAZIL'S LABOR FORCE

- Services 34%
- Agriculture 24%
- Industry 42%

The Andes are the highest mountains in the Western Hemisphere. The tallest peaks are over 23,000 feet (7000m). The Andes extend along the entire western coast of South America.

SOUTH AMERICA:
Cross Section of the Continent

ELEVATION

Meters	Feet
Over 6000	Over 20,000
3000 to 6000	10,000 to 20,000
1500 to 3000	5,000 to 10,000
600 to 1500	2,000 to 5,000
300 to 600	1,000 to 2,000
150 to 300	500 to 1,000
0 to 150	0 to 500
Below sea level	Below sea level

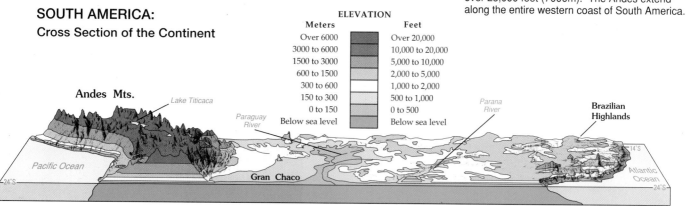

Andes Mts. • Lake Titicaca • Paraguay River • Gran Chaco • Parana River • Brazilian Highlands • Pacific Ocean • Atlantic Ocean

ARCTIC

Lofoten Is.

ICELAND
Reykjavik⊗
Surtsey I.
▲Hekla
1491m

N

NORWEGIAN SEA

ARCTIC CIRCLE

PRIME MERIDIAN

N O R W A Y

S w e d e n

Trondheims Fiord

Faeroe Islands

Rockall

Shetland Islands

Sogne Fiord
Hardanger Fiord

Bokna Fiord

Oslo⊗

L. Malaren

H e b r i d e s

Orkney Is.

Grampian Mts.

NORTH SEA

Skagerrak

Gotland

Kattegat

IRELAND
Irish Sea
GREAT BRITAIN
UNITED KINGDOM

Cambrian Mts.

London⊗

British Isles

DENMARK
Jutland

Copenhagen⊗

Gotaland

Bornholm

Baltic

TO RUSSIA

ATLANTIC

O C E A N

Celtic Sea

English Channel
Strait of Dover

Frisian Is.

Elbe R.

N o r t h e r n

GERMANY

P O L A

Warsaw⊗

Channel Is.

NETHERLANDS

BELGIUM

Seine R.

LUXEMBOURG

Ore Mts.

CZECH REPUBLIC

Elbe R.

Vistula

Carpa

SLOVAKI

Paris⊗

Paris Basin

F R A N C E

Loire R.

Danube R.

Munich●

SWITZERLAND

LIECH.

AUSTRIA

HUNGARY

Cape Finisterre

Bay of Biscay

Aquitaine Basin

Massif Central

Mt. Blanc
4807m▲

A l p s

Rhone R.

SLOVENIA

Great Hungari

Cantabrian Mts.

Duero R.

Pyrenees

ANDORRA

MONACO

SAN MARINO

CROATIA

BOSNIA

Lisbon⊗

PORTUGAL

Ebro R.

Douro R.

SPAIN

Tagus R.

Madrid⊗

Iberian

Guadiana

Gulf of Lion

Ligurian Sea

Corsica

VATICAN CITY

Rome⊗

Apennines

Adriatic Sea

D i n a r i

YUGOSLAVIA

Cape St. Vincent

Peninsula

Guadalquivir

Balearic Sea

ITALY

Vesuvius
1277m▲

MACEDON

A l p

Strait of Gibraltar

■GIBRALTAR (U.K.)

Balearic Islands

Sardinia

Tyrrhenian Sea

Gulf of Taranto

ALBANIA

Pindus

G R

Algiers⊗

M E D I T E R R A N E A N

Sicily

Ionian Sea

Ionian Is.

MOROCCO

A F R I C A

ALGERIA

Tunis⊗

TUNISIA

MALTA
Maltese Islands

Peloponnesus

WESTERN SAHARA

OCEAN
North Cape
Barents Sea
Novaya Zemlya
Kolguyev I.
Kanin Pen.
Pechora Basin
L. Inari
Lapland
Kola Pen.
FINLAND
White Sea
Archangel
Lake Region
L. Onega
Lake Ladoga
RUSSIA
Ural Mountains
Kamskoye Res.
Kama Upland
Gulf of Finland
St. Petersburg (Leningrad)
ESTONIA
Peipus
Rybinsk Res.
Gorkii Res.
Volga R.
Kuybyshev Res.
Tyuterya R.
Kama R.
Riga
LATVIA
Moscow
LITHUANIA
Central
Nieman R.
European
Russian
Oka R.
Oka-Don
Volga Upland
KAZAKHSTAN
ASIA
BELARUS
Upland
Plain
Ural R.
Pripyat Marshes
Plain
Volgograd Res.
Dnepr
Lowland
Volgograd Res.
Caspian Depression
Aral Sea
Syr Darya
UZBEKISTAN
UKRAINE
Volga R. Delta
Amu Darya
Dnestr R.
Dnepr R.
MOLDOVA
Sea
Lowland
Sea of Azov
Caspian
ROMANIA
Odessa
Black
Crimea Pen.
Caucasus Mountains
Mt. Elbrus 5642m
Sea
TURKMENISTAN
Transylvanian Alps
Bucharest
Danube
Black Sea
GEORGIA
Baku
Balkan Mts.
BULGARIA
Balkan Peninsula
Bosporus
Istanbul
Sea of Marmara
ARMENIA
AZERBAIJAN
Caspian Sea
Olympus 2917m
Dardanelles
Euboea
TURKEY
Lake Van
Lake Urmia
Tehran
Cyclades
Sporades
L. Tuz
Rhodes
SEA
IRAN
Crete
CYPRUS
SYRIA
IRAQ
LEBANON

EUROPE
Physical

————	International boundary
---------	Other boundary
⊗ Copenhagen	National capital
● Odessa	Major city

ELEVATION

Meters	Feet
Over 3000	Over 10,000
1500 to 3000	5,000 to 10,000
600 to 1500	2,000 to 5,000
300 to 600	1,000 to 2,000
150 to 300	500 to 1,000
0 to 150	0 to 500
Below sea level	Below sea level

WATER DEPTH

Less than 200	Less than 600
Greater than 200	Greater than 600

0 100 200 300 400 500 Miles

0 100 200 300 400 500 Kilometers

Complete legend on page 5

EUROPE
Political

BOUNDARIES

International boundary

Internal boundary

Other boundary
(disputed or undefined)

CITIES

● Barcelona   A city's relative size is
● Liverpool   shown by the size of
· Constanta   its symbol and lettering.

⊛ Moscow   National capital

0   100   200   300   400   500 Miles

0   100 200 300 400 500 Kilometers

Complete legend on page 5

OCEAN

Barents Sea

Novaya Zemlya

Kolguyev I.

Hammerfest
Vardo

Murmansk

L. Inari

Kiruna

White Sea

Archangel

Oulu

FINLAND

Gulf of Bothnia

Vaasa

Onega R.

Northern Dvina R.

Sukhona R.

RUSSIA

Syktyvkar

Pechora R.

Ob R.

L. Onega

Kamskoye Res.

Tampere
Turku
Helsinki

L. Saimaa

Lake Ladoga

Gulf of Finland

Perm

St. Petersburg
(Leningrad)

Tallinn

ESTONIA

L. Peipus

Rybinsk Res.

Yaroslavl

Gorki Res.

Kama R.

Vyatka R.

Kuybyshev Res.

Kazan

Ufa

Riga

LATVIA

Pskov

Volga R.

Moscow

Nizhniy Novgorod

Volga R.

Oka R.

LITHUANIA

Western Dvina R.

Vilnius

Neman R.

Minsk

BELARUS

Dvina R.

Tula

Samara

Orenburg

Bryansk

Orel

Don R.

Saratov

Oral

Ural R.

KAZAKHSTAN

Pripyat Marshes

Pripyat R.

Chernobyl

Voronezh

Volgograd Res.

ASIA

Bug R.

Kiev

Kharkiv

Donets R.

Dnepr R.

Lviv

UKRAINE

Dnestr R.

Dnipropetrovsk

Donetsk

Don R.

Volgograd

Volga R.

Syr Darya

Aral Sea

UZBEKISTAN

Prut R.

MOLDOVA
Chisinau

Rostov-on-Don

Astrakhan

Amu Darya

Cluj-Napoca

Odessa

Sea of Azov

Kerch

Novorossiysk

Krasnodar

Grozny

Volga R. Delta

TURKMENISTAN

ROMANIA

Sevastopol

Caspian Sea

Bucharest

Danube

Constanta

Black Sea

Sofia

Varna

GEORGIA

Tbilisi

Baku

Ashgabat

BULGARIA

Plovdiv

ARMENIA
Yerevan

AZERBAIJAN

Bosporus

Istanbul

Sea of Marmara

Caspian Sea

Salonika

Dardanelles

TURKEY

Euboea

Ankara

L. Tuz

Lake Van

Lake Urmia

Tehran

Athens

IRAN

Aegean Sea

SEA

Nicosia

SYRIA

IRAQ

Crete (Greece)

CYPRUS

LEBANON

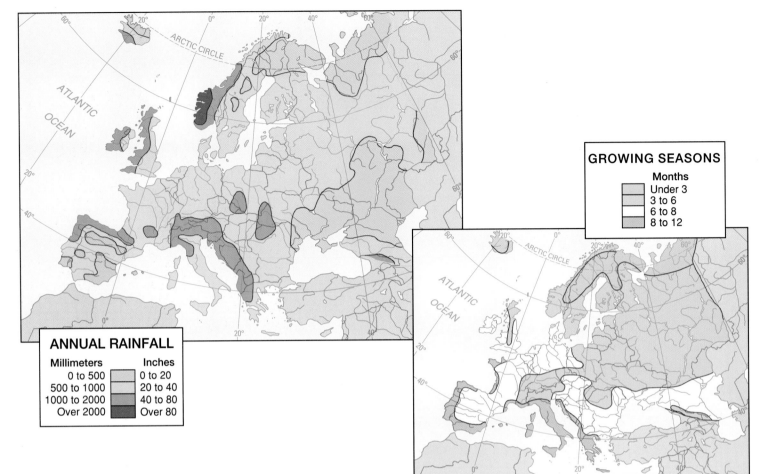

GROWING SEASONS

Months
- Under 3
- 3 to 6
- 6 to 8
- 8 to 12

ANNUAL RAINFALL

Millimeters	Inches
0 to 500	0 to 20
500 to 1000	20 to 40
1000 to 2000	40 to 80
Over 2000	Over 80

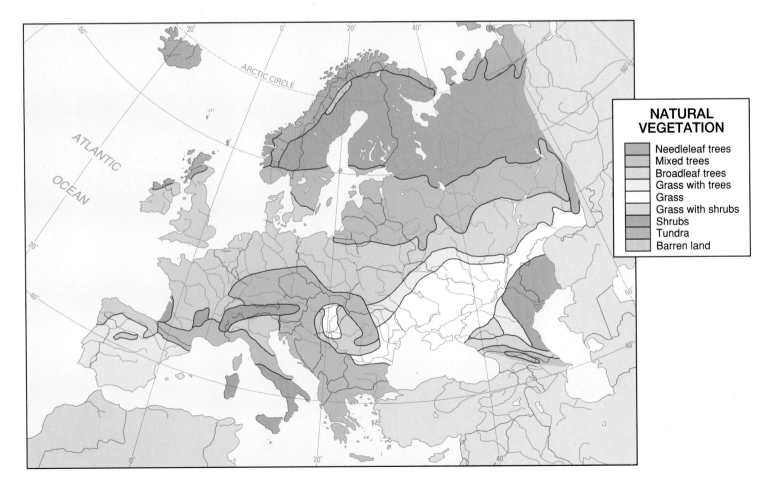

NATURAL VEGETATION

- Needleleaf trees
- Mixed trees
- Broadleaf trees
- Grass with trees
- Grass
- Grass with shrubs
- Shrubs
- Tundra
- Barren land

For centuries, Europeans considered themselves to be at the center of the known world. Through exploration and trade, they spread their influence to many other lands.

Europe is the second-smallest continent and occupies just one-fifth of the Eurasian landmass. But only Asia is more densely populated.

Madrid is Spain's capital and its largest city. Like most of Europe, Spain is highly urbanized. Over 90 percent of the Spanish people live in cities.

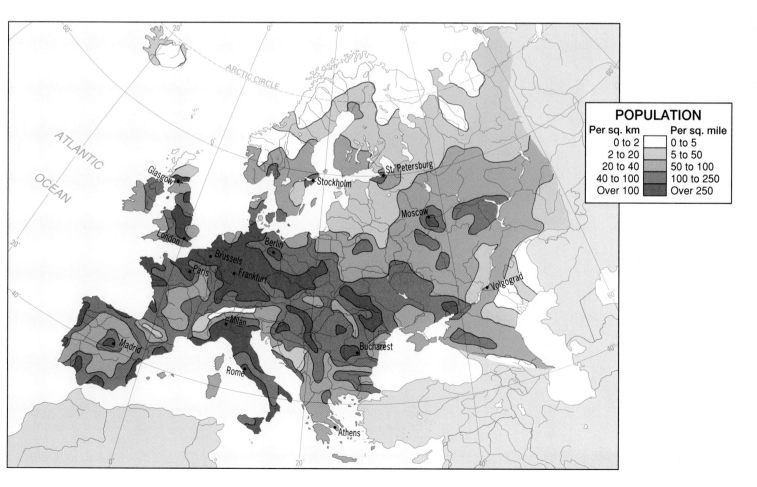

POPULATION	
Per sq. km	Per sq. mile
0 to 2	0 to 5
2 to 20	5 to 50
20 to 40	50 to 100
40 to 100	100 to 250
Over 100	Over 250

Barge on the Rhine River

RHINE RIVER

The Rhine River is the most important inland waterway in Western Europe. Several smaller rivers flow into the Rhine, and other rivers are connected to it by canals. The Rhine and the rivers flowing into it form a network of waterways. They provide water for industrial processes and cheap transportation for raw materials and manufactured goods. The Rhine itself is the busiest river in the network.

CHANGING BOUNDARIES

In 1918 the country that came to be known as Yugoslavia was formed. It united several nationalities and regions. But they began to break apart again in 1991. Four Yugoslav republics voted to become independent nations: Slovenia, Croatia, Macedonia, and Bosnia and Herzegovina.

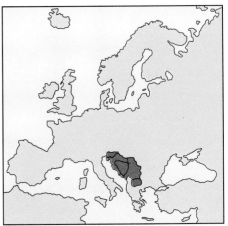

Yugoslavia and its former republics are in Southern Europe.

YUGOSLAVIA AND ITS FORMER REPUBLICS

——————	International boundary
——————	Republic boundary
- - - - -	Province boundary
• Bitola	Major city
⊛ Ljubljana	National capital
★ Novi Sad	Republic or province capital

Complete legend on page 5

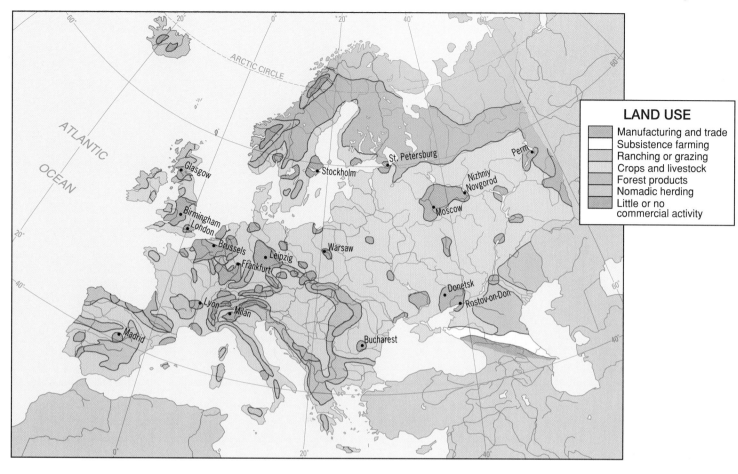

LAND USE

- Manufacturing and trade
- Subsistence farming
- Ranching or grazing
- Crops and livestock
- Forest products
- Nomadic herding
- Little or no commercial activity

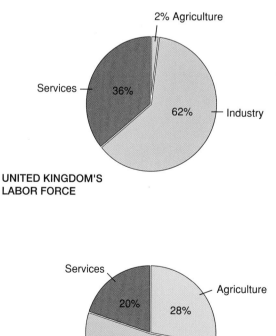

UNITED KINGDOM'S LABOR FORCE

- 2% Agriculture
- Services 36%
- Industry 62%

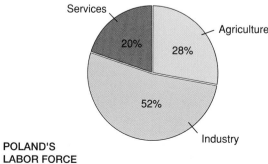

POLAND'S LABOR FORCE

- Services 20%
- Agriculture 28%
- Industry 52%

The Eiffel Tower was built for the 1889 World's Fair in Paris. The 984 foot (300 m) iron tower has become a symbol of France.

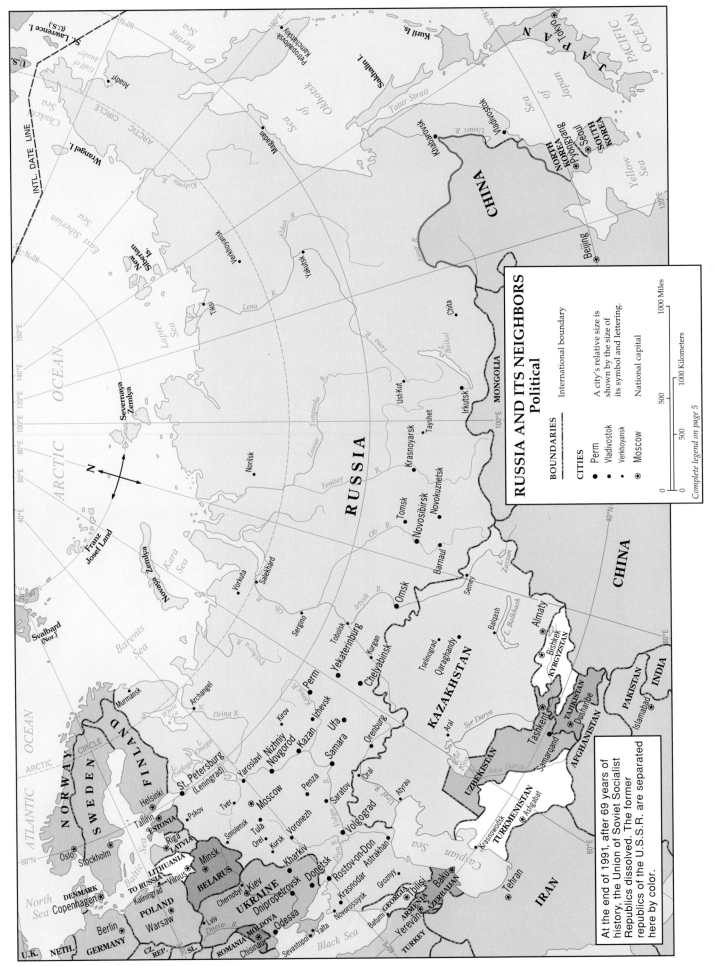

RUSSIA AND ITS NEIGHBORS
Political

BOUNDARIES International boundary

CITIES
● Perm A city's relative size is shown by the size of its symbol and lettering.
• Vladivostok
• Verkhoyansk
⊛ Moscow National capital

Complete legend on page 5

1000 Miles
1000 Kilometers
500
500

At the end of 1991, after 69 years of history, the Union of Soviet Socialist Republics dissolved. The former republics of the U.S.S.R. are separated here by color.

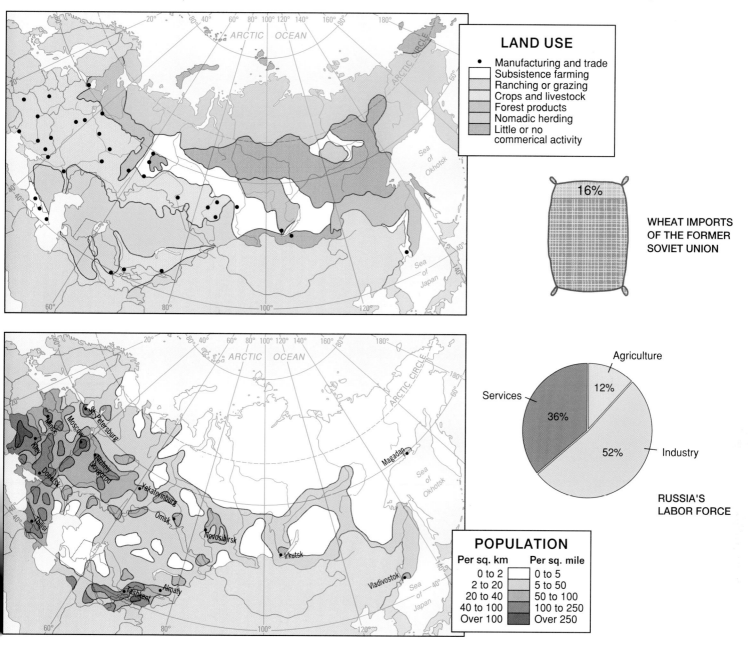

LAND USE

- • Manufacturing and trade
- Subsistence farming
- Ranching or grazing
- Crops and livestock
- Forest products
- Nomadic herding
- Little or no commerical activity

16%

WHEAT IMPORTS OF THE FORMER SOVIET UNION

Agriculture

Services 36%

12%

52% Industry

RUSSIA'S LABOR FORCE

POPULATION

Per sq. km	Per sq. mile
0 to 2	0 to 5
2 to 20	5 to 50
20 to 40	50 to 100
40 to 100	100 to 250
Over 100	Over 250

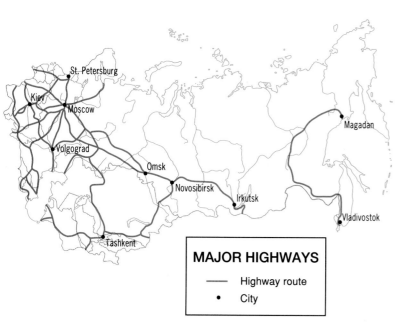

MAJOR HIGHWAYS

— Highway route

• City

Moscow is the capital of Russia, and Red Square is near the center of the city. Lining the square are the Kremlin, at the left, and the Cathedral of St. Basil, with the onion-shaped domes, Russia's most familiar landmarks.

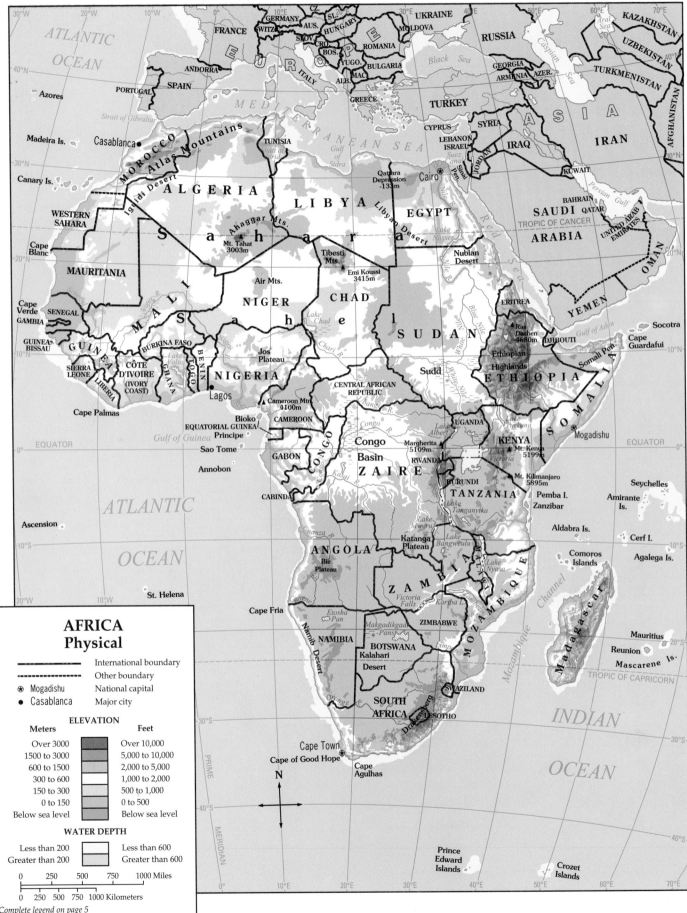

AFRICA
Physical

———	International boundary
---------	Other boundary
⊛ Mogadishu	National capital
• Casablanca	Major city

ELEVATION

Meters	Feet
Over 3000	Over 10,000
1500 to 3000	5,000 to 10,000
600 to 1500	2,000 to 5,000
300 to 600	1,000 to 2,000
150 to 300	500 to 1,000
0 to 150	0 to 500
Below sea level	Below sea level

WATER DEPTH

Less than 200	Less than 600
Greater than 200	Greater than 600

0   250   500   750   1000 Miles

0   250   500   750   1000 Kilometers

Complete legend on page 5

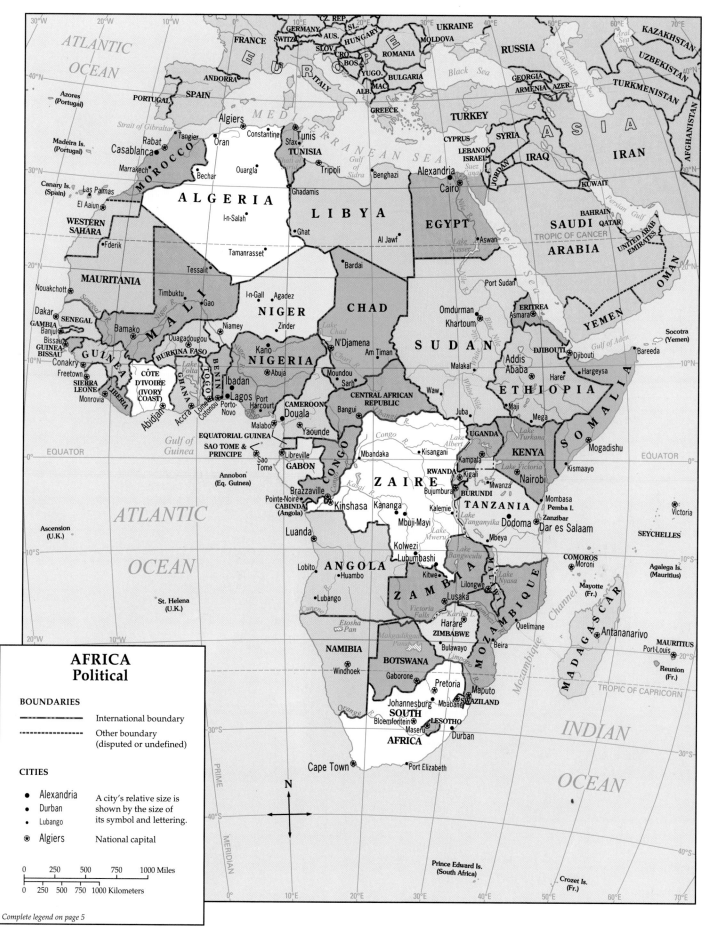

AFRICA
Political

BOUNDARIES

—————————— International boundary

------------------ Other boundary
(disputed or undefined)

CITIES

● Alexandria

• Durban

· Lubango

⊛ Algiers

A city's relative size is
shown by the size of
its symbol and lettering.

National capital

0   250   500   750   1000 Miles

0   250 500 750 1000 Kilometers

Complete legend on page 5

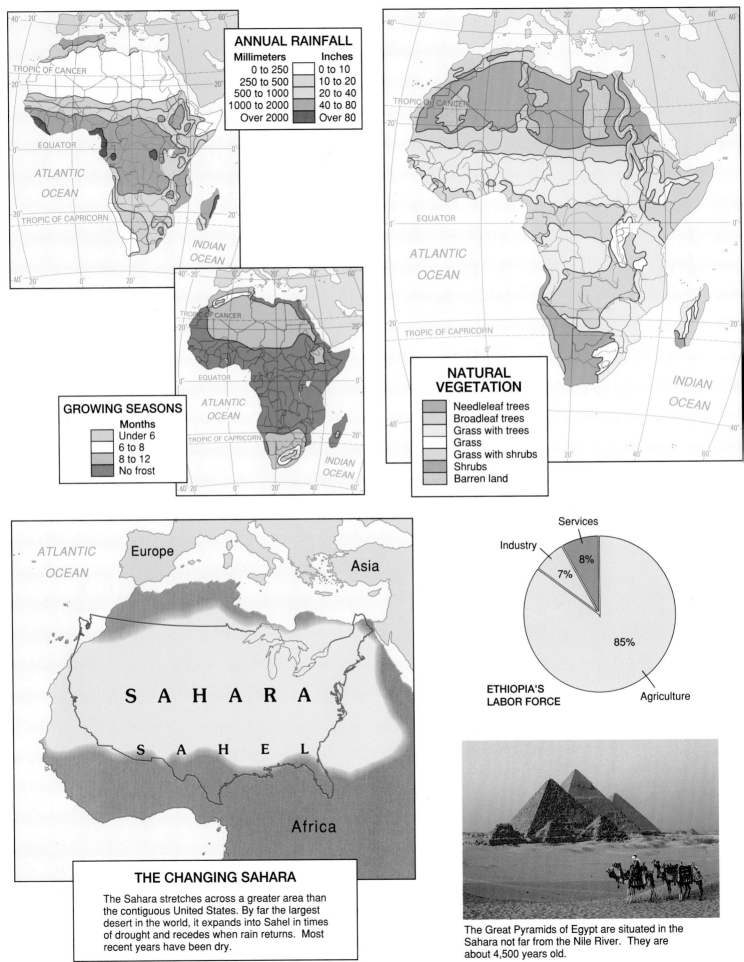

ANNUAL RAINFALL

Millimeters	Inches
0 to 250	0 to 10
250 to 500	10 to 20
500 to 1000	20 to 40
1000 to 2000	40 to 80
Over 2000	Over 80

GROWING SEASONS

Months
- Under 6
- 6 to 8
- 8 to 12
- No frost

NATURAL VEGETATION

- Needleleaf trees
- Broadleaf trees
- Grass with trees
- Grass
- Grass with shrubs
- Shrubs
- Barren land

ETHIOPIA'S LABOR FORCE

Services 8%
Industry 7%
85%
Agriculture

THE CHANGING SAHARA

The Sahara stretches across a greater area than the contiguous United States. By far the largest desert in the world, it expands into Sahel in times of drought and recedes when rain returns. Most recent years have been dry.

The Great Pyramids of Egypt are situated in the Sahara not far from the Nile River. They are about 4,500 years old.

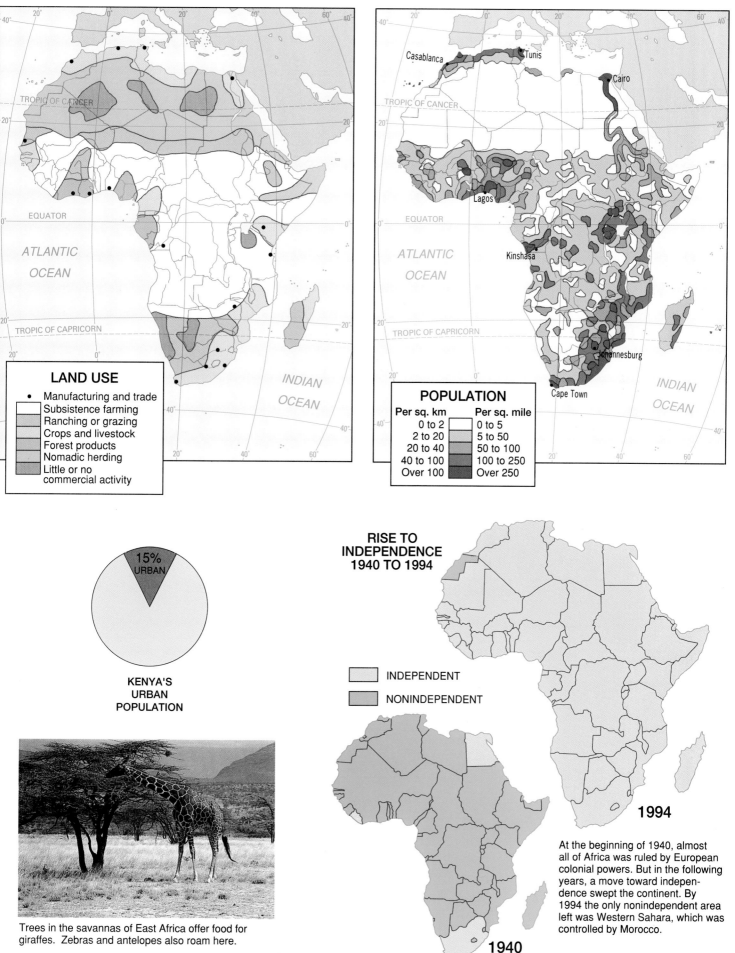

LAND USE

- • Manufacturing and trade
- Subsistence farming
- Ranching or grazing
- Crops and livestock
- Forest products
- Nomadic herding
- Little or no commercial activity

POPULATION

Per sq. km	Per sq. mile
0 to 2	0 to 5
2 to 20	5 to 50
20 to 40	50 to 100
40 to 100	100 to 250
Over 100	Over 250

15% URBAN

KENYA'S URBAN POPULATION

Trees in the savannas of East Africa offer food for giraffes. Zebras and antelopes also roam here.

RISE TO INDEPENDENCE 1940 TO 1994

- INDEPENDENT
- NONINDEPENDENT

1994

1940

At the beginning of 1940, almost all of Africa was ruled by European colonial powers. But in the following years, a move toward independence swept the continent. By 1994 the only nonindependent area left was Western Sahara, which was controlled by Morocco.

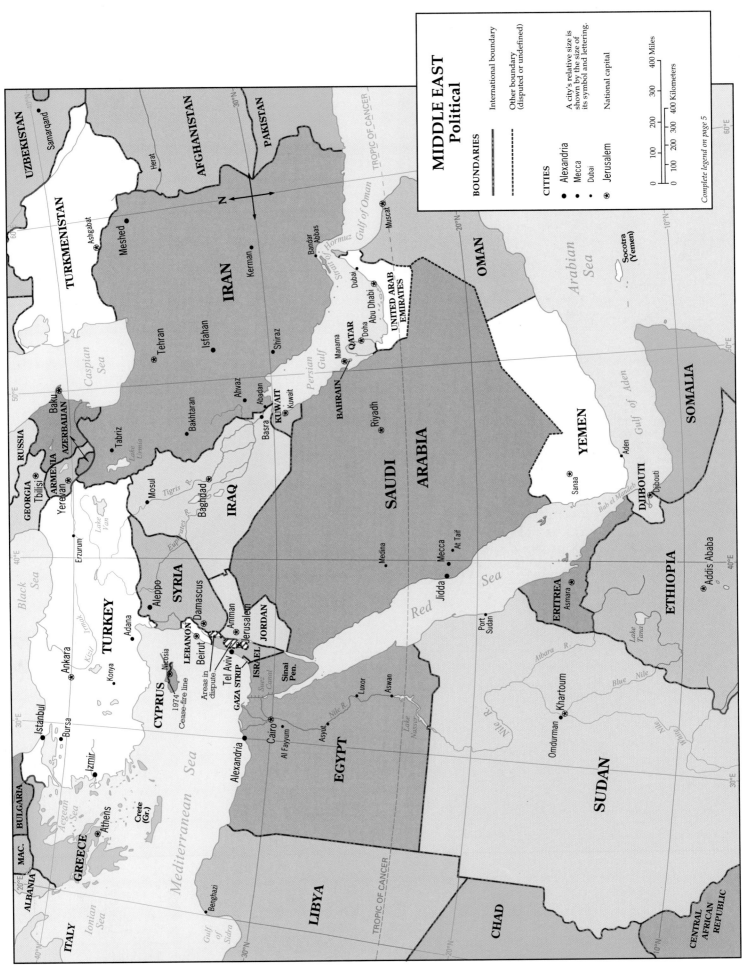

**MIDDLE EAST
Political**

BOUNDARIES

International boundary

Other boundary
(disputed or undefined)

CITIES

● Alexandria   A city's relative size is
● Mecca   shown by the size of
• Dubai   its symbol and lettering.
⊛ Jerusalem   National capital

0   100   200   300   400 Miles

0   100   200   300   400 Kilometers

Complete legend on page 5

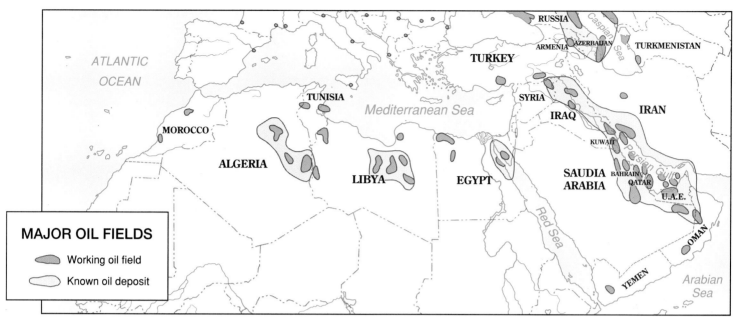

MAJOR OIL FIELDS

- Working oil field
- Known oil deposit

LEADING PETROLEUM PRODUCERS

Almost one-third of the world's petroleum is produced by OPEC.* OPEC members include the Persian Gulf countries of Iran, Iraq, Kuwait, Qatar, Saudi Arabia, and the United Arab Emirates. Other OPEC members are Algeria, Libya, Nigeria, Gabon, Indonesia, and Venezuela.

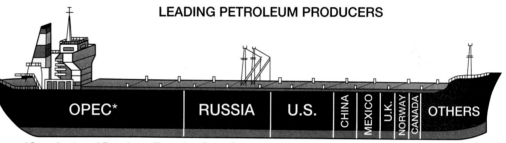

OPEC* | RUSSIA | U.S. | CHINA | MEXICO | U.K. | NORWAY | CANADA | OTHERS

*Organization of Petroleum Exporting Countries

CHANGING BOUNDARIES

Israel occupied the area shown in dark green until 1967. After the Six Day War of that year, it also controlled the parts of Egypt, Jordan, and Syria shown in light green.

In stages during 1975, 1979, and 1982, Israel returned the Sinai Peninsula to Egypt. But Israel remained in control of the Gaza Strip, West Bank, and Golan Heights.

In 1993 Israeli and Palestinian leaders signed an agreement that would lead to self-rule for Palestinians living in Gaza and the city of Jericho.

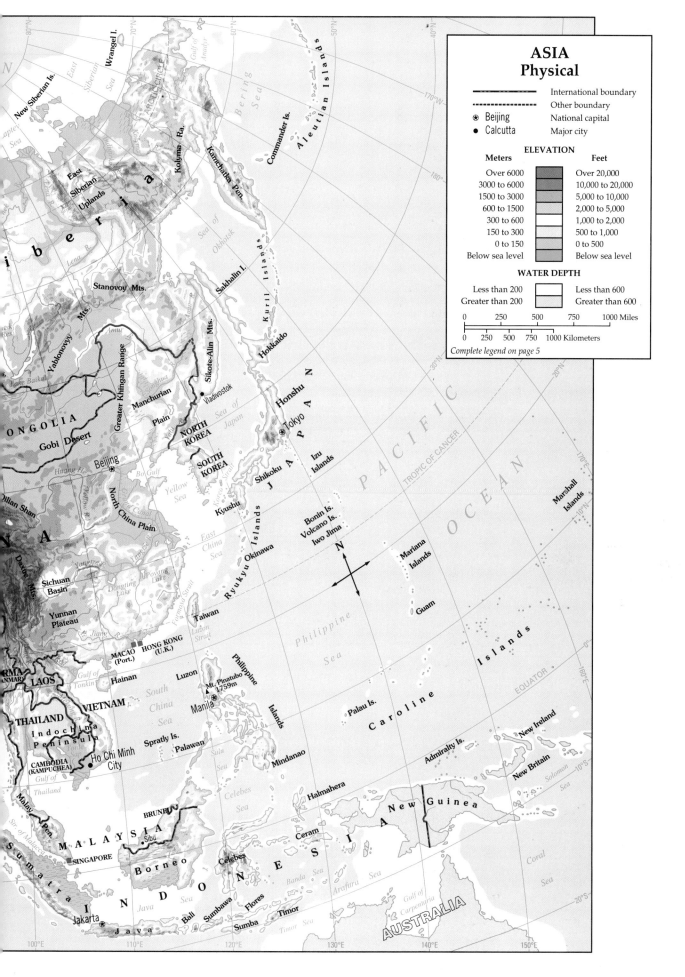

ASIA
Physical

———————	International boundary
- - - - - - - -	Other boundary
⊛ Beijing	National capital
● Calcutta	Major city

ELEVATION

Meters		Feet
Over 6000		Over 20,000
3000 to 6000		10,000 to 20,000
1500 to 3000		5,000 to 10,000
600 to 1500		2,000 to 5,000
300 to 600		1,000 to 2,000
150 to 300		500 to 1,000
0 to 150		0 to 500
Below sea level		Below sea level

WATER DEPTH

Less than 200		Less than 600
Greater than 200		Greater than 600

0   250   500   750   1000 Miles

0   250   500   750   1000 Kilometers

Complete legend on page 5

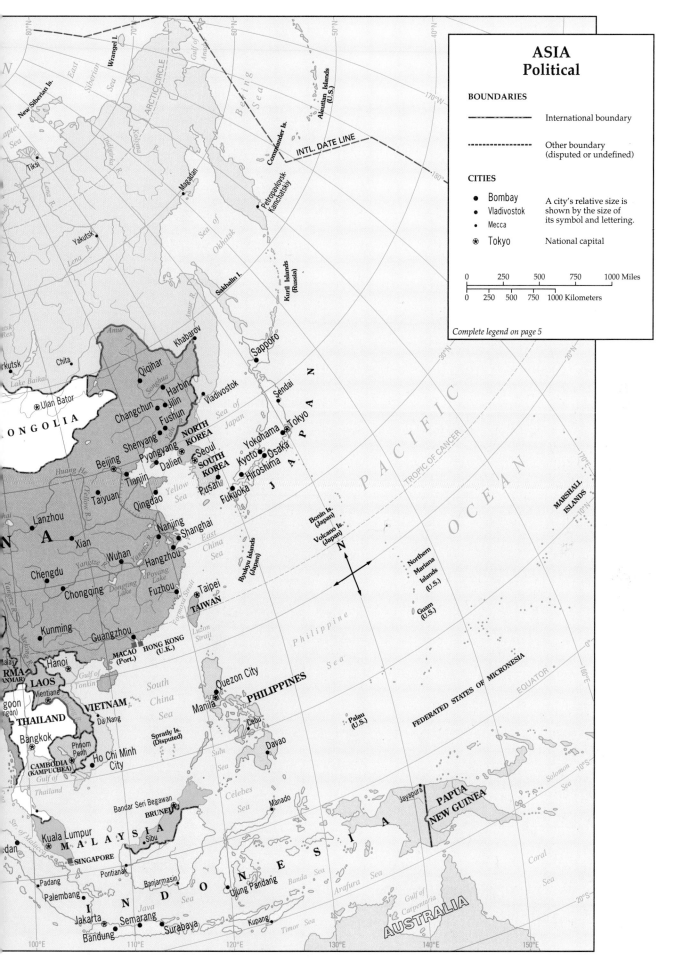

ASIA
Political

BOUNDARIES

— — — — — International boundary

- - - - - - - - - - Other boundary
(disputed or undefined)

CITIES

● Bombay   A city's relative size is
● Vladivostok   shown by the size of
• Mecca   its symbol and lettering.
⊛ Tokyo   National capital

```
0      250    500    750    1000 Miles
0   250  500  750  1000 Kilometers
```

Complete legend on page 5

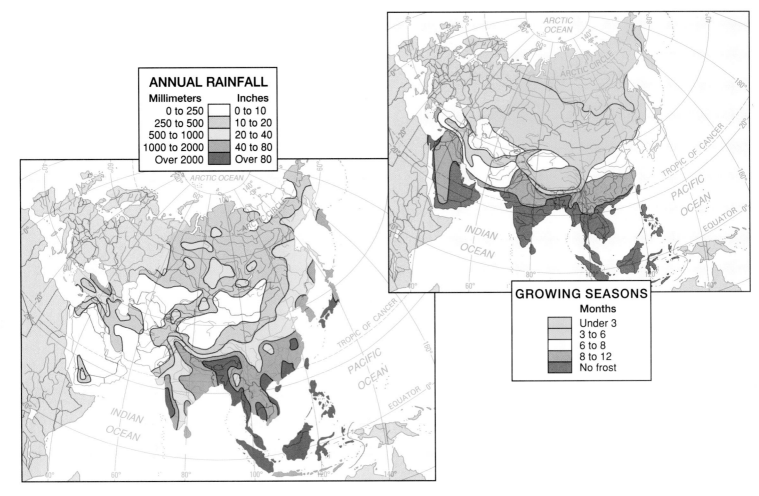

ANNUAL RAINFALL

Millimeters	Inches
0 to 250	0 to 10
250 to 500	10 to 20
500 to 1000	20 to 40
1000 to 2000	40 to 80
Over 2000	Over 80

GROWING SEASONS

Months
Under 3
3 to 6
6 to 8
8 to 12
No frost

ASIA
Cross Section of the Continent

ELEVATION

Meters		Feet
Over 6000		Over 20,000
3000 to 6000		10,000 to 20,000
1500 to 3000		5,000 to 10,000
600 to 1500		2,000 to 5,000
300 to 600		1,000 to 2,000
150 to 300		500 to 1,000
0 to 150		0 to 500
Below sea level		Below sea level

The Himalaya Mountains are the world's tallest. Often called "the Roof of the World," they rise as high as 29,028 feet (8848 m).

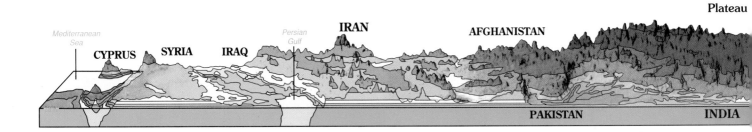

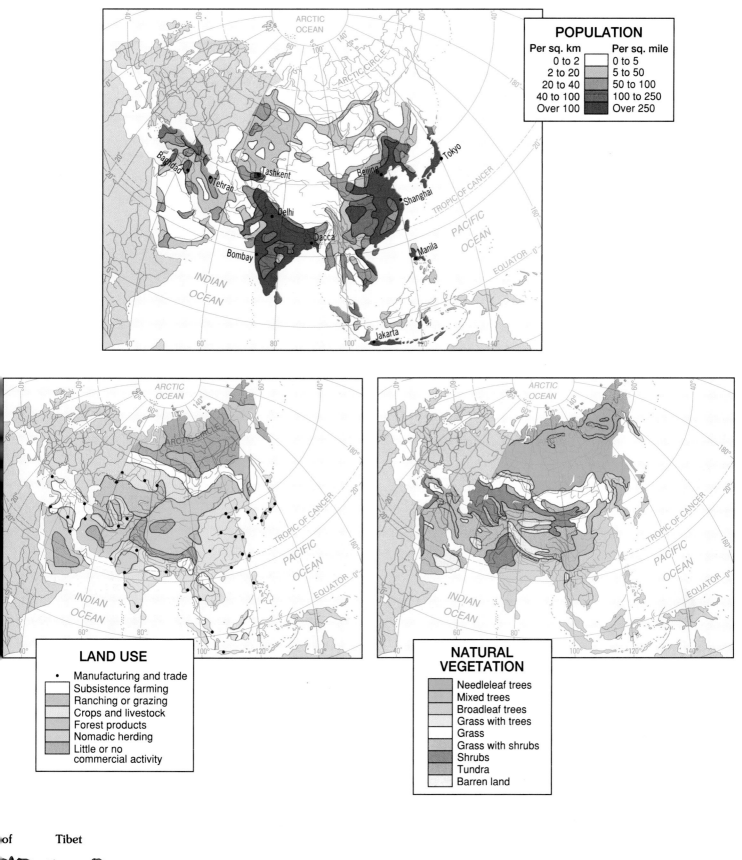

POPULATION

Per sq. km	Per sq. mile
0 to 2	0 to 5
2 to 20	5 to 50
20 to 40	50 to 100
40 to 100	100 to 250
Over 100	Over 250

Baghdad
Tehran
Tashkent
Beijing
Tokyo
Shanghai
Delhi
Dacca
Bombay
Manila
Jakarta

ARCTIC OCEAN
ARCTIC CIRCLE
TROPIC OF CANCER
PACIFIC OCEAN
EQUATOR
INDIAN OCEAN

LAND USE

- Manufacturing and trade
- Subsistence farming
- Ranching or grazing
- Crops and livestock
- Forest products
- Nomadic herding
- Little or no commercial activity

NATURAL VEGETATION

- Needleleaf trees
- Mixed trees
- Broadleaf trees
- Grass with trees
- Grass
- Grass with shrubs
- Shrubs
- Tundra
- Barren land

of Tibet

CHINA

KOREA

JAPAN

Yellow Sea

Pacific Ocean

36°N

28°N

CHINA:
Population and Landscape

· One dot represents
100,000 people

⊛ National capital

— International boundary

ᴧᴧᴧ Great wall

The Great Wall of China was built about 2,200 years ago to defend the country against invaders. It remains the world's longest structure and extends across 1,500 miles (2415 km) of northern China.

HONG KONG'S LABOR FORCE

- 1% Agriculture
- Services 20%
- Industry 79%

CHINA'S LABOR FORCE

- Services 5%
- Industry 24%
- Agriculture 71%

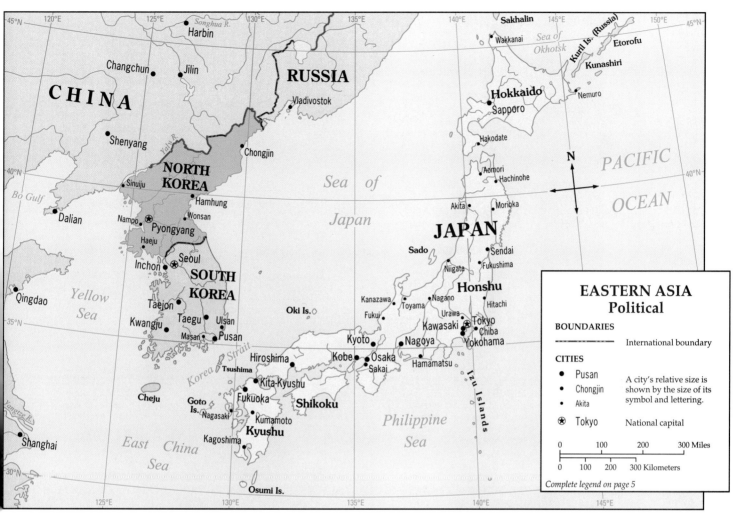

EASTERN ASIA
Political

BOUNDARIES

——————— International boundary

CITIES

● Pusan

• Chongjin

· Akita

⊛ Tokyo   National capital

A city's relative size is shown by the size of its symbol and lettering.

0   100   200   300 Miles

0   100   200   300 Kilometers

Complete legend on page 5

JAPAN'S TRADE

Japan exports 30% more goods than it imports.

EXPORT DESTINATIONS

United States

Germany

South Korea

Taiwan

Hong Kong

Singapore

United Kingdom

Australia

Canada

All other countries

IMPORT SOURCES

United States

China

South Korea

Australia

Indonesia

Germany

Saudi Arabia

Taiwan

Canada

France

All other countries

77% URBAN

JAPAN'S URBAN POPULATION

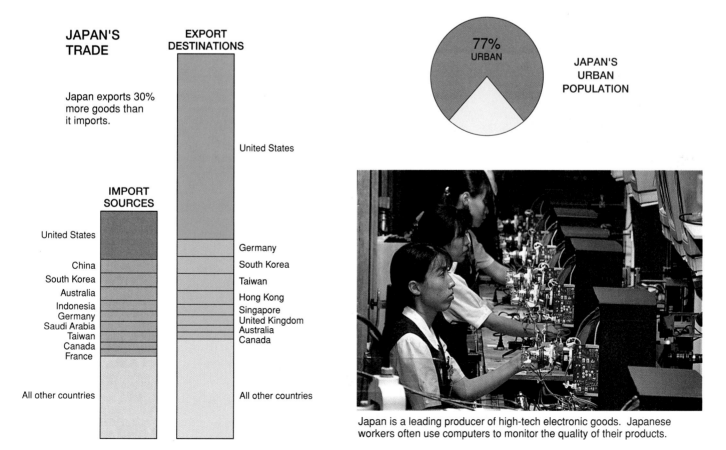

Japan is a leading producer of high-tech electronic goods. Japanese workers often use computers to monitor the quality of their products.

INDIA'S SIZE AND SHAPE

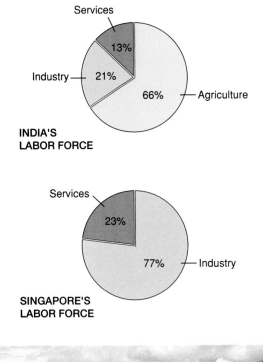

India	1,222,243 sq. mi. (3 165 596 sq. km)
48 States	3,021,295 sq. mi. (7 825 112 sq. km)

India is only about one-third the size of the United States. But it has the second largest population in the world, about three and one-half times as many people as the United States has.

INDIA'S LABOR FORCE

Services 13%
Industry 21%
Agriculture 66%

SINGAPORE'S LABOR FORCE

Services 23%
Industry 77%

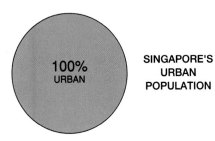

100% **URBAN**

SINGAPORE'S URBAN POPULATION

Millions of Asians grow rice, the continent's most important food crop. China and India account for more than one-half the rice produced in the world.

INDONESIA'S POPULATION

- One dot represents 75,000 people
- Major city
- ⊛ National capital

THAILAND
PHILIPPINES
South China Sea
Medan
Kuala Lumpur
Bandar Seri Begawan
BRUNEI
Celebes Sea
MALAYSIA
PACIFIC OCEAN
SINGAPORE
Padang
Borneo
Halmahera
Sumatra
Celebes
Palembang
Java Sea
Ceram
I N D O N E S I A
New Guinea
Jakarta
Semarang
Ujung Pandang
Banda Sea
INDIAN OCEAN
Bandung
Surabaya
Java
Yogyakarta
Malang
Timor
Arafura Sea
Surakarta
Timor Sea
AUSTRALIA

SIX ASIAN COUNTRIES

Six Asian countries are home for nearly half of the world's population. But the 2,600,000,000 people living there occupy less than 12% of the world's land area.

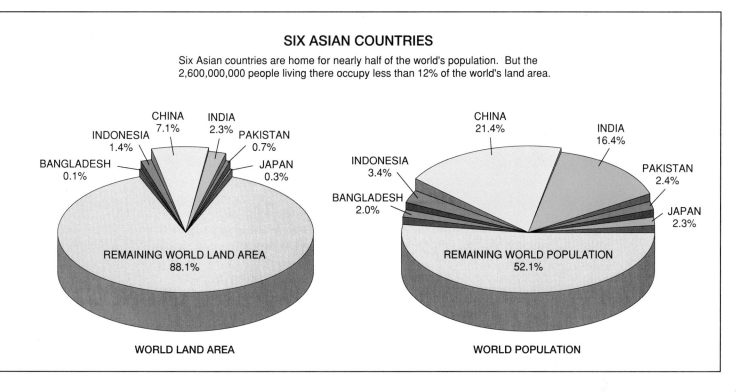

WORLD LAND AREA

INDONESIA 1.4%
BANGLADESH 0.1%
CHINA 7.1%
INDIA 2.3%
PAKISTAN 0.7%
JAPAN 0.3%
REMAINING WORLD LAND AREA 88.1%

WORLD POPULATION

CHINA 21.4%
INDIA 16.4%
INDONESIA 3.4%
BANGLADESH 2.0%
PAKISTAN 2.4%
JAPAN 2.3%
REMAINING WORLD POPULATION 52.1%

MONSOON ASIA

The climate of Southeastern Asia and India is dominated by seasonal wind systems called **monsoons**. The word *monsoon* is derived from the Arabic term *mausim*, meaning "season." The arrival of the wet monsoon is vital to the success of crops that feed half of the world's people.

Dry Monsoon

In winter, dry winds generated over the cold surface of the land blow toward the warmer oceans and keep clouds away. But when winter ends, the mainland warms up faster than the oceans, and the winds shift.

Wet Monsoon

In summer, the monsoon changes from dry to wet as the winds reverse direction. Cooler air over the oceans rushes toward warm land, bringing massive amounts of moisture that produce rain. The region's growing season occurs with the wet monsoon.

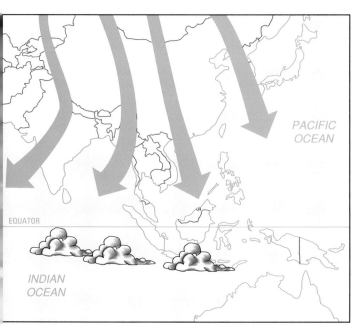

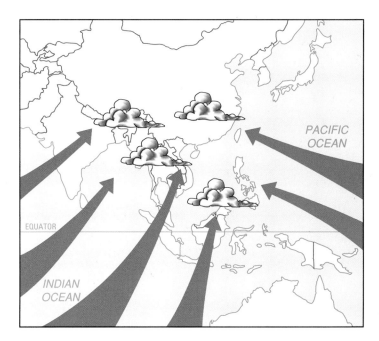

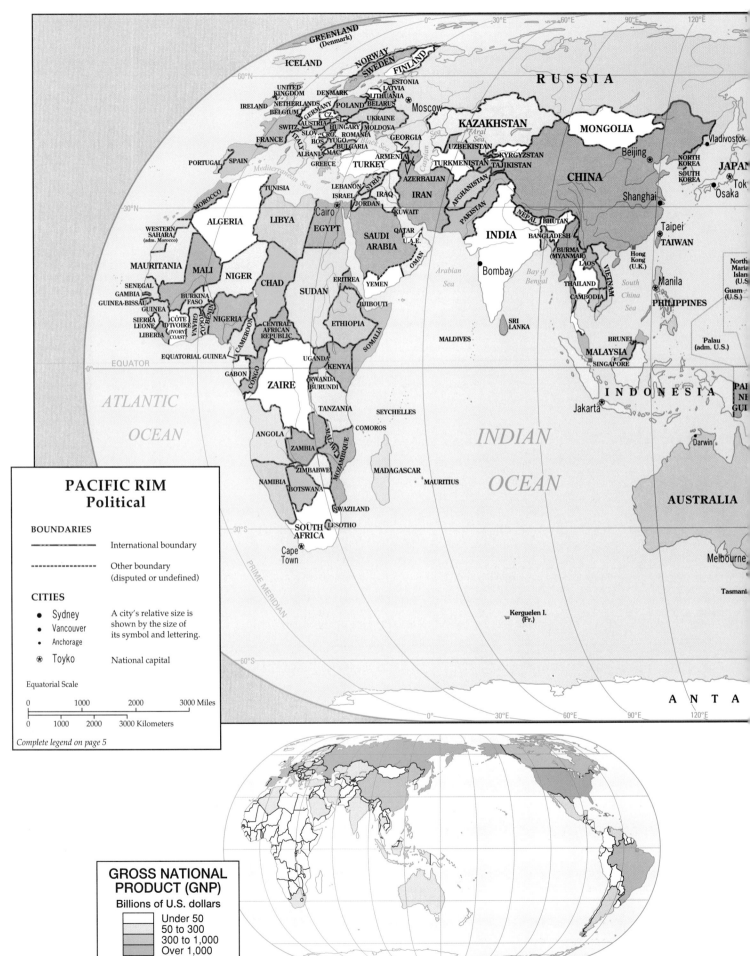

PACIFIC RIM
Political

BOUNDARIES

———————	International boundary
- - - - - - - -	Other boundary (disputed or undefined)

CITIES

● Sydney — A city's relative size is shown by the size of its symbol and lettering.
● Vancouver
• Anchorage
⊛ Toyko — National capital

Equatorial Scale

0   1000   2000   3000 Miles
0   1000   2000   3000 Kilometers

Complete legend on page 5

GROSS NATIONAL PRODUCT (GNP)
Billions of U.S. dollars

☐	Under 50
☐	50 to 300
☐	300 to 1,000
☐	Over 1,000

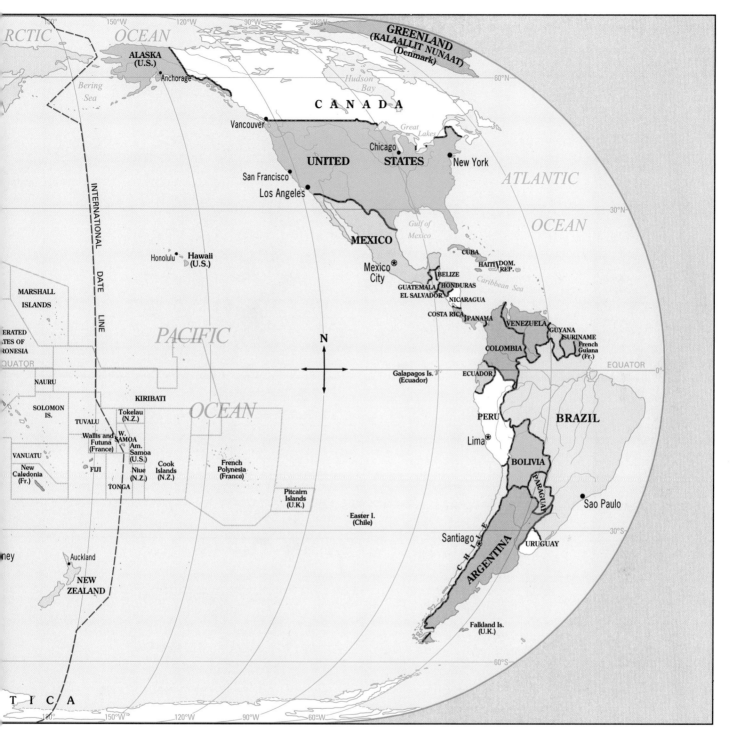

ARCTIC OCEAN

GREENLAND
(KALAALLIT NUNAAT)
(Denmark)

ALASKA
(U.S.)

Anchorage

Bering
Sea

60°N

CANADA

Vancouver

Great
Lakes

Hudson
Bay

UNITED   STATES

Chicago

New York

San Francisco

ATLANTIC

Los Angeles

30°N

OCEAN

MEXICO

Gulf of
Mexico

Honolulu   Hawaii
(U.S.)

CUBA

HAITI   DOM.
REP.

MARSHALL
ISLANDS

Mexico
City

BELIZE

FEDERATED
STATES OF
MICRONESIA

GUATEMALA   HONDURAS
EL SALVADOR

Caribbean Sea

PACIFIC

NICARAGUA

NAURU

COSTA RICA   PANAMA

VENEZUELA

GUYANA
SURINAME
French
Guiana
(Fr.)

EQUATOR

KIRIBATI

COLOMBIA

EQUATOR   0°

Galapagos Is.
(Ecuador)

ECUADOR

SOLOMON
IS.

Tokelau
(N.Z.)

OCEAN

PERU

BRAZIL

TUVALU

Wallis and
Futuna
(France)

W.
SAMOA
Am.
Samoa
(U.S.)

Cook
Islands
(N.Z.)

French
Polynesia
(France)

Lima

VANUATU

New
Caledonia
(Fr.)

FIJI

Niue
(N.Z.)

BOLIVIA

TONGA

Pitcairn
Islands
(U.K.)

Sao Paulo

PARAGUAY

Easter I.
(Chile)

30°S

Sydney

Auckland

Santiago

CHILE

ARGENTINA

URUGUAY

NEW
ZEALAND

Falkland Is.
(U.K.)

60°S

ANTARCTICA

N

INTERNATIONAL DATE LINE

180°   150°W   120°W   90°W   60°W

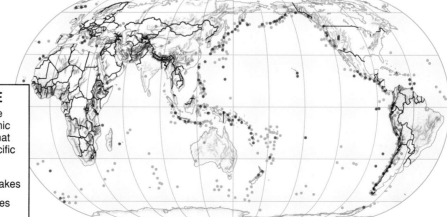

RING OF FIRE

The "ring of fire" is the
belt of frequent volcanic
and seismic activity that
encompasses the Pacific
Ocean.

- ⋯ Major earthquakes
- ⋯ Major volcanoes

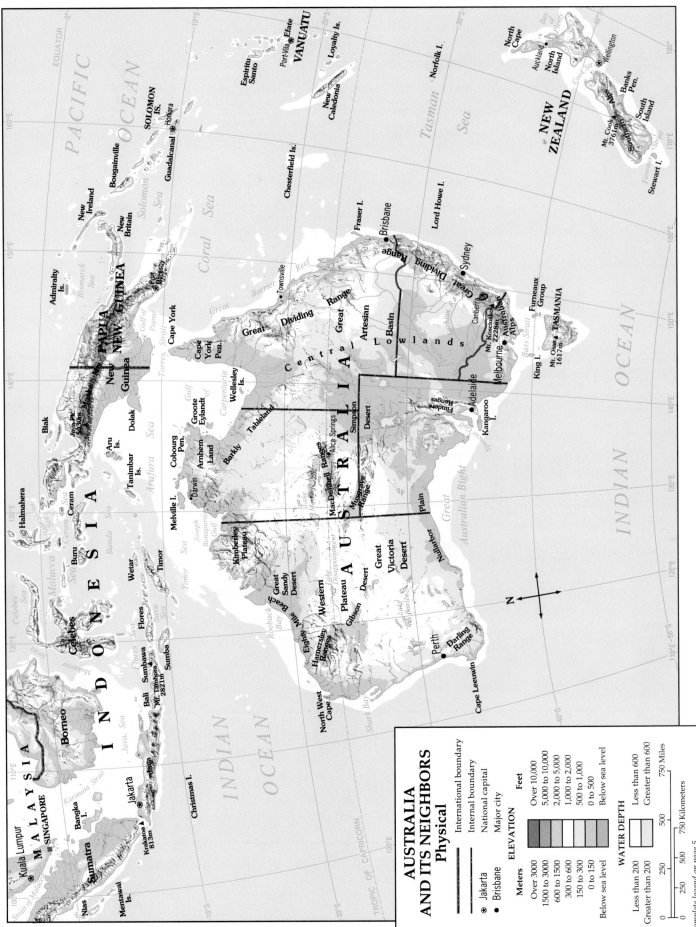

AUSTRALIA AND ITS NEIGHBORS
Physical

International boundary
Internal boundary

⊛ Jakarta   National capital
● Brisbane   Major city

ELEVATION

Meters		Feet
Over 3000		Over 10,000
1500 to 3000		5,000 to 10,000
600 to 1500		2,000 to 5,000
300 to 600		1,000 to 2,000
150 to 300		500 to 1,000
0 to 150		0 to 500
Below sea level		Below sea level

WATER DEPTH

Less than 200	Less than 600
Greater than 200	Greater than 600

0   250   500   750 Miles

0   250   500   750 Kilometers

Complete legend on page 5

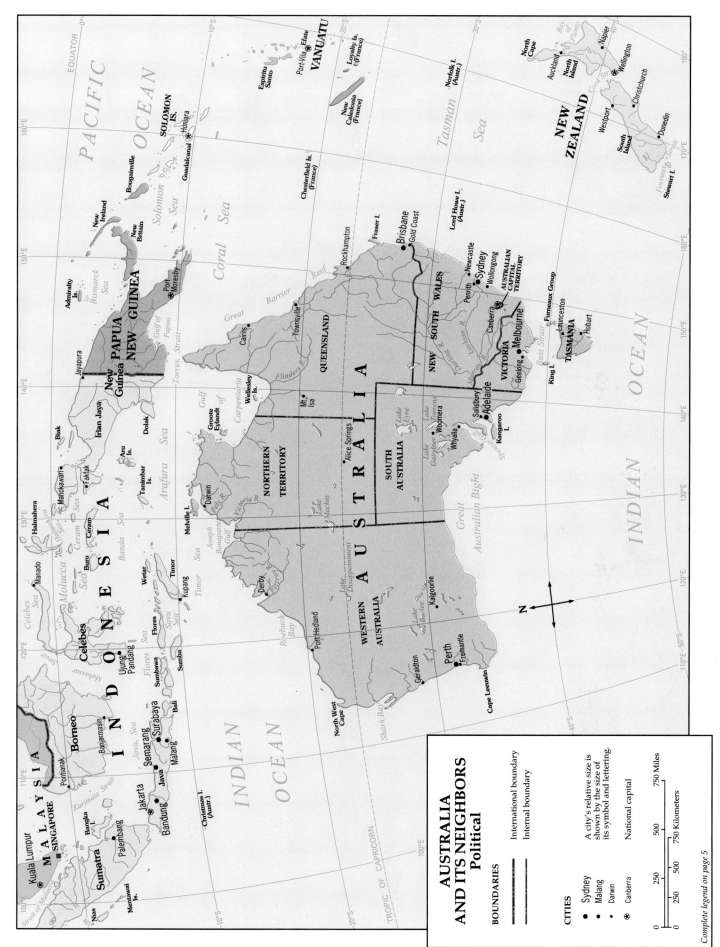

AUSTRALIA
AND ITS NEIGHBORS
Political

BOUNDARIES

—————— International boundary

—————— Internal boundary

CITIES

A city's relative size is
shown by the size of
its symbol and lettering.

• Sydney

• Malang

• Darwin

⊛ Canberra   National capital

0   250   500   750 Miles

0   250   500   750 Kilometers

Complete legend on page 5

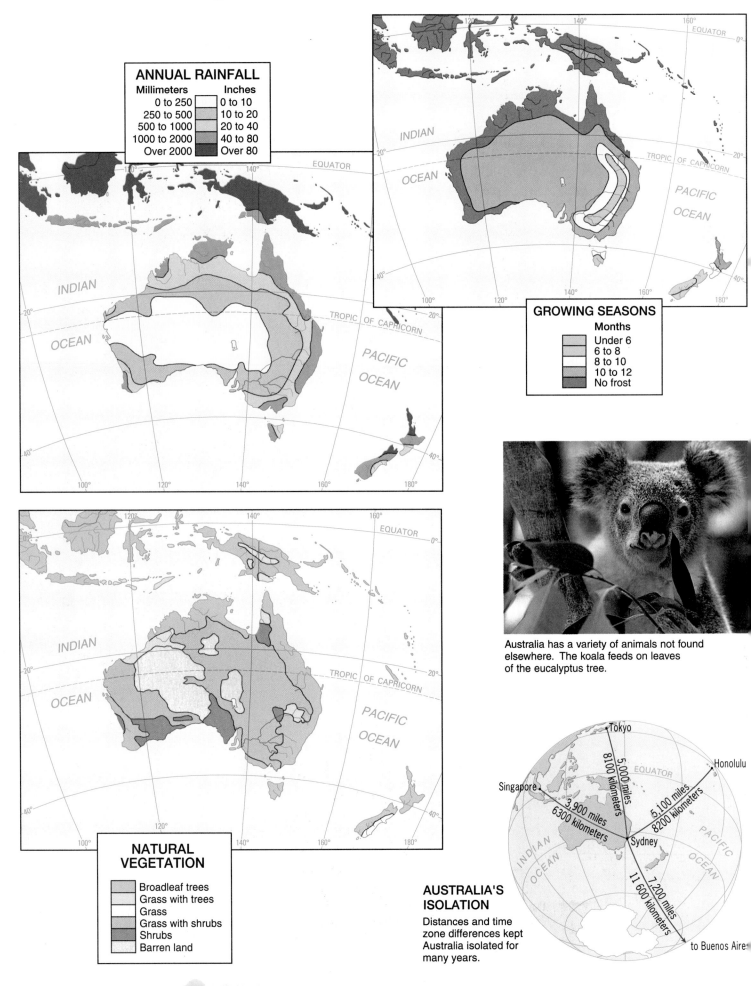

ANNUAL RAINFALL

Millimeters	Inches
0 to 250	0 to 10
250 to 500	10 to 20
500 to 1000	20 to 40
1000 to 2000	40 to 80
Over 2000	Over 80

GROWING SEASONS

Months
- Under 6
- 6 to 8
- 8 to 10
- 10 to 12
- No frost

NATURAL VEGETATION

- Broadleaf trees
- Grass with trees
- Grass
- Grass with shrubs
- Shrubs
- Barren land

Australia has a variety of animals not found elsewhere. The koala feeds on leaves of the eucalyptus tree.

AUSTRALIA'S ISOLATION

Distances and time zone differences kept Australia isolated for many years.

LAND USE

- Manufacturing and trade
- Subsistence farming
- Ranching or grazing
- Crops and livestock
- Forest products
- Little or no commercial activity

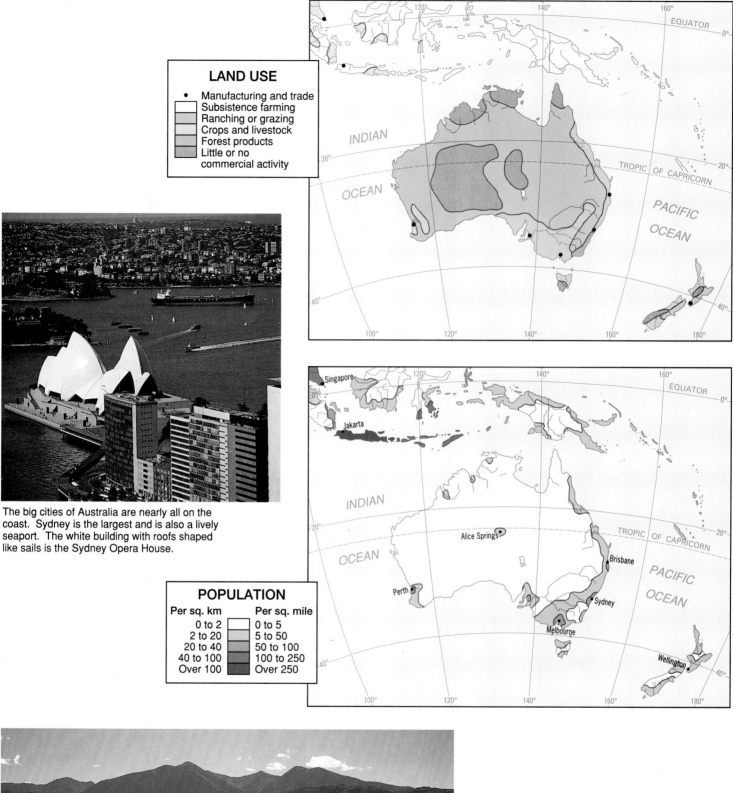

The big cities of Australia are nearly all on the coast. Sydney is the largest and is also a lively seaport. The white building with roofs shaped like sails is the Sydney Opera House.

POPULATION

Per sq. km	Per sq. mile
0 to 2	0 to 5
2 to 20	5 to 50
20 to 40	50 to 100
40 to 100	100 to 250
Over 100	Over 250

Sheep are central to the agriculture of both Australia and New Zealand. These two countries are the world's leading exporters of wool.

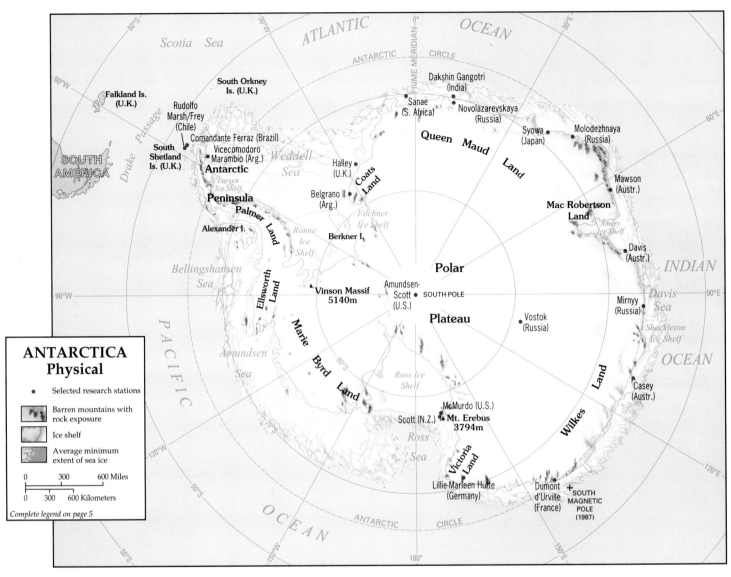

ANTARCTICA
Physical

- • Selected research stations
- Barren mountains with rock exposure
- Ice shelf
- Average minimum extent of sea ice

0	300	600 Miles
0	300	600 Kilometers

Complete legend on page 5

Penguins can withstand extreme cold and are excellent divers and swimmers. They are numerous along the coast of Antarctica. But only insects live in the harsh Antarctic interior.

ANTARCTICA'S ICE CAP

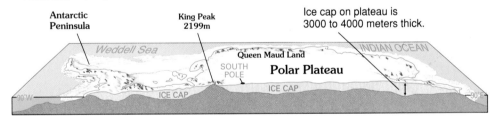

Antarctic Peninsula

King Peak 2199m

Ice cap on plateau is 3000 to 4000 meters thick.

Weddell Sea

Queen Maud Land

SOUTH POLE

Polar Plateau

INDIAN OCEAN

ICE CAP

ICE CAP

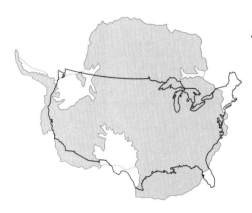

ANTARCTICA: THE COLD CONTINENT

- • Antarctica is almost twice the size of the contiguous United States.
- • Antarctica also is much larger than Australia and Europe.
- • 98% of Antarctica is covered by ice and snow.
- • Antarctica's ice cap has a volume of 7.25 million cubic miles (30 million cubic kilometers).
- • Antarctica's ice cap contains 70% of the world's fresh water supply.

EARTH NOTES

AGE
4,600,000,000 years

WEIGHT
6,600,000,000,000,000,000,000 tons
(5.9 x 10^{21} metric tons)

6.6 SEXTILLION TONS

EQUATORIAL DIAMETER
7,926.41 miles
(12 756 kilometers)

POLAR DIAMETER
7,899.83 miles
(12 713.5 kilometers)

EQUATORIAL CIRCUMFERENCE
24,901.55 miles
(40 075 kilometers)

POLAR CIRCUMFERENCE
24,859.82 miles
(40 008 kilometers)

LAND SURFACE AREA
57,259,000 sq. mi.
(148 300 000 sq. km)
or 29% of total surface area

WATER SURFACE AREA
139,692,000 sq. mi.
(361 800 000 sq. km)
or 71% of total surface area

HIGHEST TEMPERATURE
136°F (58°C) at Al Aziziyah, Libya
September 13, 1922

LOWEST TEMPERATURE
−129°F (−89°C) at Vostok, Antarctica
July 21, 1983

ROTATION
Spinning of Earth on its axis,
once every 23 hr., 56 m., 4.09 sec

REVOLUTION
Earth's journey around the sun,
once every 365 days, 6 hr., 9 m., 9.54 sec.

HIGHEST POINT ON LAND
Mt. Everest, Asia
29,028 ft. (8848 m) above sea level

LOWEST POINT ON LAND
Shore of Dead Sea, Asia
1,312 ft. (400 m) below sea level

DEEPEST POINT IN OCEAN
Mariana Trench, Pacific Ocean
36,198 ft. (11 033 m) below sea level

MOST RAIN
Mt. Waialeale, Hawaii
460 in. (11 684 mm) yearly average

LEAST RAIN
Arica, Chile
0.02 in. (0.5 mm) yearly average

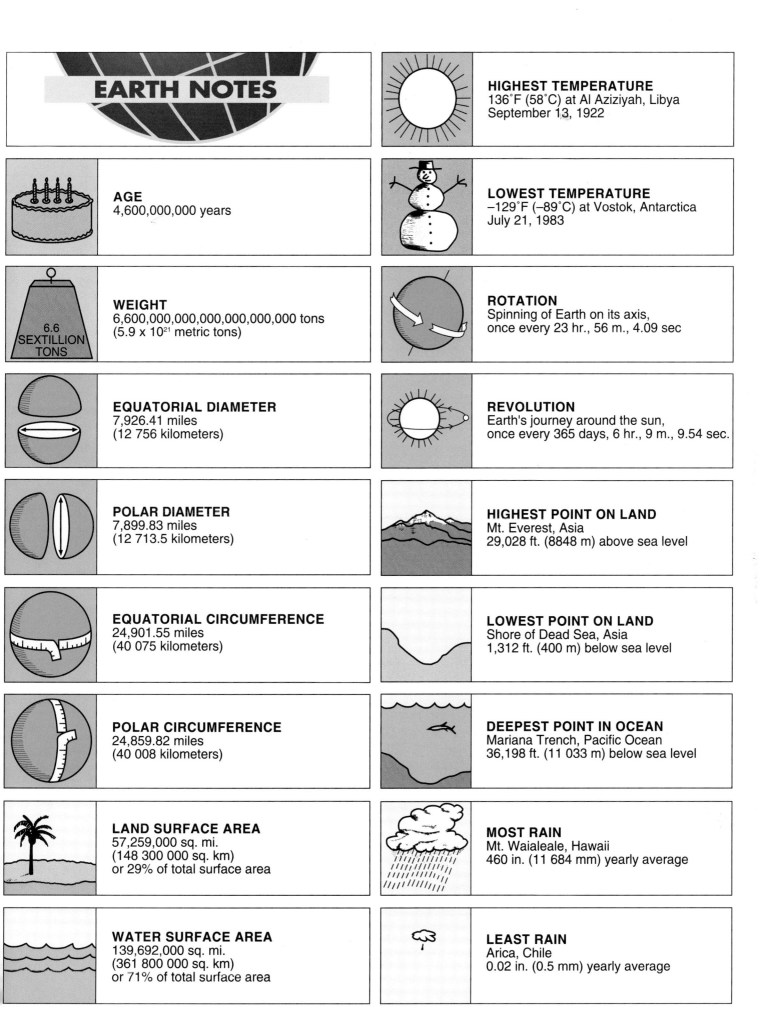

WORLD MAP PROJECTIONS

Map projections are the means by which the curved surface of a globe is transferred to the flat surface of a map. Because the earth is a sphere, a globe is its only perfect model. Even though there are an infinite number of map projections, none can be as accurate as a globe. A globe simultaneously shows accurate shapes, sizes, distances, and directions. No single world map can show all four of these properties accurately. Every world map distorts one or more of them. For example, a world map that shows correct shapes cannot show correct sizes, and vice versa.

The projections illustrated here can be classified according to their map properties. *Conformal* projections show true shapes, but distort sizes. (You can remember this term's meaning by associating *shape* with the word *form* in *conformal*.) *Equal-area* projections show all areas in their true relative sizes, but distort shapes. *Compromise* projections allow some size distortions in order to portray shapes more accurately. For all types of world map projections, distortion is generally least near the center of the map and greatest at its edges.

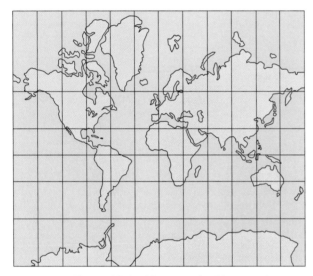

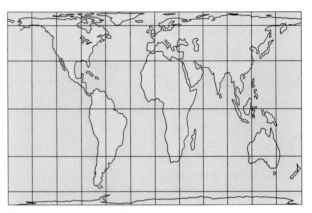

Gall-Peters: An equal-area projection first produced in the 1850s, the Gall-Peters greatly distorts shapes near the Equator as well as near the poles. Features near the Equator are stretched vertically, while features near the poles are flattened horizontally. The resulting shapes are quite different from those on the globe.

Mercator: First published in 1569, the Mercator is a conformal projection. North and South Poles are shown not as points, but as lines the same length as the Equator. The result is extreme size distortion in the higher latitudes. The Mercator map was designed for navigation, and the true compass direction between any two points can be determined by a straight line.

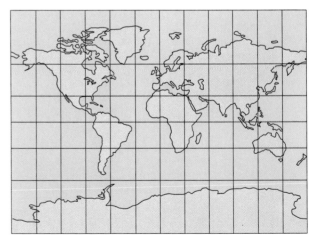

Armadillo: The Armadillo is a compromise projection that is intended to give young students the impression of a map being peeled from a globe. Because its unique appearance results in severe distortions, especially at the map's outer edges, it has seldom been used outside the classroom.

Miller Cylindrical: The Miller is a compromise projection based on the Mercator. Its shapes are not as accurate as those on the Mercator map, but it has much less size distortion in the higher latitiudes. The Miller cylindrical projection is frequently used when mapping world time zones.

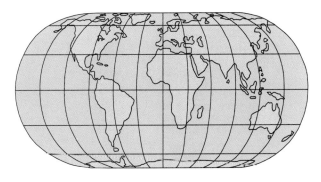

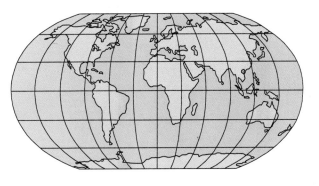

Eckert IV: An equal-area projection, the Eckert IV has relatively minor shape distortions near the Equator and the poles. The result is a map that is well-suited either for general reference or for showing world distributions. It has been used in several atlases to show world climates and other themes.

Robinson: First used in 1963, the Robinson is a compromise projection. Because it presents a reasonable overall picture of the world, it is often used for maps in educational materials. It looks similar to the Eckert IV (at left), but the Robinson is easily distinguished by its distortion in the polar areas.

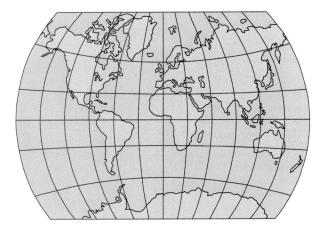

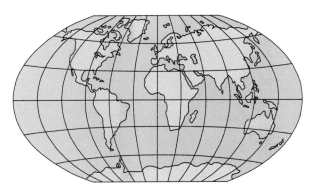

Van der Grinten: The Van der Grinten is a compromise between the Mercator (at left) and the Mollweide (below). The full projection is shaped like a circle, but the polar areas are normally not shown. Shapes and directions are reasonably accurate between 60°N and 60°S, where most of the world's people live. The Van der Grinten has long been used for general reference maps.

Winkel "Tripel": The Winkel "Tripel" is a compromise projection. Its oval shape and curving parallels result in a map with realistic shapes and minor size distortions at all latitudes. The Winkel has less size distortion than the Van der Grinten (at left) and less shape distortion than the Robinson (above).

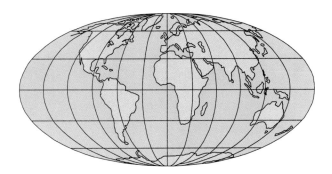

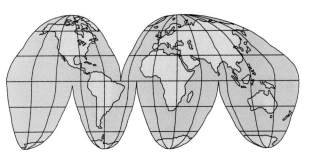

Mollweide: An equal-area projection, the Mollweide has an oval shape that reminds the viewer of a globe. The Mollweide projection is frequently used for world distribution maps. (A distribution map shows the relative location and extent of something—such as crops, livestock, or people—across the face of the earth.)

Goode's Homolosine: Goode's is an equal-area projection that also shows shapes extremely well. Shapes can be shown more accurately than on most equal-area maps because the grid is *interrupted* or split in the ocean areas. The interruptions allow land areas to be shown with less stretch or distortion.

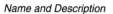

INDEX